TRACES OF

WISDOM

TRACES OF WISDOM

Amish Women and the Pursuit
of Life's Simple Pleasures

louise stoltzfus

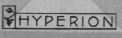

NEW YORK

See page 355 for reprint acknowledgments

Book design by Nicola Ferguson

For information address
Hyperion, 114 Fifth Avenue,
New York, New York 10011.

Library of Congress Cataloging-in-Publication Data
Stoltzfus, Louise.
Traces of wisdom : Amish women and the pursuit of life's simple pleasures /
Louise Stoltzfus. — 1st ed.
p.   cm.
ISBN 0-7868-6323-4
1. Amish women.   2. Women—Conduct of life.   I. Title.
BX8129.A5S84   1997
305.48'687—dc21   97-34321

FIRST EDITION

10 9 8 7 6 5 4 3 2 1

To my family.

You are all here.

You are the source of all that

sustains and blesses my life.

Acknowledgments

My deepest appreciation and thanks to the Amish women who so graciously gave me their time as I worked on this project. Many are women I have known throughout my life. I thank them sincerely for the solid foundation of hope and grace that has become the basis for my life's work. I shall be forever grateful.

Many names have been changed to protect my people and their privacy. While I had conversations with women in several other Amish communities, most of my inspiration and material came from the Amish women of Lancaster County, Pennsylvania. This is true because Lancaster County is my home, and these are my people.

I thank my family and friends for supporting me through both the exhilarating and intimidating stages of this writing. In particular, I thank Ruth Ann Meyers Kulp, who read and responded to various drafts of the manuscript during our Wednesday morning meetings over coffee and pastries.

I thank my agent, Scott Waxman, for his thoughtful and patient work in the early stages of this project. I could not have done it without you. Thank you.

I also thank my editor, Gretchen Young, for her guidance and perceptions throughout the preparation and completion of this book. I could not have found a better match for refining its expressions and ideas. Thank you.

Contents

CONTENTS

CONTENTS

❀ ❀

CONTENTS

❀ ❀

xi

CONTENTS

❧ ❧

TRACES OF

WISDOM

I Have
Come Home

I have been Amish. I have lived in the warm cocoon of kindness spun by a large family complete with parents, eleven brothers and sisters, grandparents, several dozen aunts and uncles, and more than one hundred cousins. I have known the care and protection of an Amish grandmother whose home was a haven of hope. I have known the gentle touch of an Amish mother's heart and hands, an Amish father's wisdom and generosity.

This is the foundation upon which my life is built. The eyes through which I see the world. The measure by which I gauge human affection and goodwill. Or the absence thereof. For the women and men who raised me believed that living well included both security and suffering, joy and sorrow, pain and pleasure. That a life of sincerity and common sense required compassion and forgiveness. That hopes and dreams were more easily fulfilled in simple ways and even passions. So it is that the essence of these people, their stories, and the rhythms of their world have found root and growth at the farthest reaches of my soul and spirit.

But I am no longer Amish. I am no longer an insider. I am no longer different from the world. I have instead become a woman of the world. My hair is short and cropped. I don't wear it, as women among my people do, long and neatly bound beneath a head covering. Strangers don't stare at me in crowded supermarkets, as they do at them. My plain dresses are all gone (except one that hangs alone at the back of my closet). I have not always kept to the standards of simplicity common to my people, to their dreams and hopes for me. I have been gone from the church of my childhood and youth for many years.

❀ ❀ ❀ ❀

Although leaving changed my actions and dreams dramatically, I have
not been able to stop thinking (or being) like an Amish woman. The
core values of my childhood have come with me to this new and
different place. They bring a rich dimension of health and grace to
my worldly soul, an open door to forgiveness and light, and the rare
gift of living in two worlds.

In the one, I dine in fine French bistros; in the other, I live on my
mother's mashed potatoes, roast beef, and old-fashioned bean soup.
In the one, I enjoy Bach, Beethoven, and Dvořák; in the other, I
prefer a cappella gospel songs and ancient German hymns. In the one,
I am a city dweller, walking the busy streets of commerce and industry;
in the other, I am a country woman, watching the sunset from the
back porch of my family home. I love both worlds with equal fervor.

I am ever and always most surprised by this dual resonance in my
soul. By how my past informs the present. By sudden flashes of memory and recognition. By the familiar nearness of an antique Amish
quilt, whether I find it in an art museum or on a bed in an Amish

home. By the instant sensation of my grandmother's oyster stew, whether it is served in my mother's home or in a seafood restaurant on the Chesapeake Bay.

These memories come to life because the museum's quilt came *from* my people, perhaps discovered in an Amish woman's attic by a researcher or collector, and the recipe came *to* my people, perhaps delivered by an eastern-shore seafood peddler driving door to door among the Lancaster County Amish.

This sort of effortless exchange is and has always been a natural part of living and being with my people. Though I am no longer Amish, it is a privilege they have also given me—to move in and out of their ideas and opinions, their spaces and homes—and it shadows everything I believe, everything I do. I cannot say "we" when I speak of Amish women, but I can and probably always will say "These are my people." For I am powerfully drawn to the spare and plain traditions that keep these women close to earth and me close to them.

Sometimes women among my people ask, "Why did you leave?" Sometimes they wonder how I have come to this place, how I have become so like the people they call "women of the world."

Who can know the mysteries of the human mind and body? Who

can know why some of us wish to be brain surgeons and poets or playwrights and professors? Who can know why others want to be teachers and nurses or mothers and homemakers? Who can know? This I ask myself and try to remember when my people inquire what force guided me from the bosom of this restful, peaceful place. My home.

Amish women make no apologies for the otherness of their lives. They ask me directly, "If you admire us so much, why did you leave?" They wonder about the experience of leaving, the reality of changing focus and reasoning in such a fundamental way. I don't always know how to answer them with honesty and integrity.

What I do know is that I have both lost and gained. Beyond the Amish world, I found wide new horizons. A whole new world with paintings and poetry, museums and theater, music and memory. A world I would be sad never to have known.

But who I am has not changed. I am still as Amish, on the inside, as I was on the day I left. Like these women, I know the earth to be a better place because of the Amish way. Like them, I also often question the wisdom of contemporary life, the fashions, inventions, and philosophies of each new decade and age. I am certain that the

Amish rejection of modernity does not signal backwardness or ignorance, but rather a powerful connection to common sense and the timeless worth of the human soul.

❧ ❧ ❧ ❧

For contrary to what the age of progress, its advertisers and adherents, would have us believe, microwave ovens and automobiles, televisions and stereo systems, beach houses and maintenance-free condominiums do not define, nor are they essential ingredients of, the good life. Amish women believe they can live well, perhaps even better, without any and all of these tokens of convenience and leisure.

Think about it. Is it not true that gas burners create more evenly cooked dinners and delicacies? Has it not been shown that public transportation not only saves energy and the environment but also money? Is it not more peaceful to fall asleep with images from a fine novel or good book, rather than those of isolated and pointless local crimes constantly thrust into our consciousness by what passes for an accounting of the day's news? Does not the human voice achieve its own soaring tones, far surpassing the disconcerting beat that has become the trademark of a good stereo system? Are not city houses with roof and window gardens or modest country homes with vast fruit and vegetable patches more neighborly than palaces of pleasure or hallway-bound apartments, warm on the inside but cold and distant on the outside?

These are questions that occur to all of us, whether or not we are Amish, when we remember how glorious it feels to partake of a carefully prepared meal. To let someone else do the driving. To read a truly fine book. To hear a great singer. To play in the dirt. They occur to us when we realize that the criteria by which we determine worth, fulfillment, self-respect, indeed the good life, must remain grounded in standards and comparisons very different from those championed by the practitioners of progress.

I believe Amish women are uniquely positioned to speak to us about avoiding the pitfalls of rampant competition and commercialism, about rising above the demands of our jobs and homes, about living with honor and respect for ourselves and for each other.

❧ ❧ ❧ ❧

"I honestly do not know how to fix this." As women of the world, most of us have cried some version of this distress call recently echoed by my friend, a soccer mom with three preteen children, a suburban home, and a full-time management position in her family business.

How to fix this? Although the Amish women I know have not been immune to overcommitment and overwork, they do seek simplicity. They hope we find the same within the parameters of our own experiences and opportunities. Even when this means we decide to leave high-pressure jobs for the sake of our children. Even when it means we give up trying to be supermoms or superwomen. Even when it means fewer social obligations, fewer hours away from home, and saying no repeatedly.

We are, all of us, women arriving at the dawn of the twenty-first century, sometimes marked and mangled by the days in which we live but essentially whole at the core and center of our souls. We may, perhaps, achieve a finer tuning with our own source of reason and seat of good judgment by internalizing the reflections, opinions, and words of Amish women.

❧ ❧ ❧ ❧

Many Amish women are as certain today—in these hours and years at the end of the century—as my grandmothers were at the beginning of the century, that they are called to different lives. To living in the world, but resolutely refusing to be of the world. To fostering friendship and helpfulness, not conflict and one-upmanship.

For through the years of the twentieth century, Amish women have stood by the men in their lives as their communities have grown by astonishing leaps and bounds. They are slowly becoming an ever-present religious group, a growing and vital segment of the North American story. One that is both admired and reviled. One that is increasingly well interpreted, but often widely misunderstood. One that seeks only to continue its ageless tradition of being "the quiet in the land." One that persists in not trying to explain itself, but often proclaims, "We are only human; we are no different than any of you."

My people have not wished for this growing scrutiny of their culture, but they try to understand and accept that numerical growth and their presence in many places arouses curiosity and questioning. Many women prefer and ask to be left alone. Many others are willing, as some have always been, to involve the world in conversation. Ever they are in the world, but never are they of the world.

For it is not disengagement from human reality that sets Amish women and their husbands and families apart. My people engage in much of the great wealth of human experience, but they also seek constantly to remind themselves that life is short. They express a simple, well-defined desire to live with freedom, hope, and dignity, but they also remember that the world in which they live, in which we all live, is a fragile place where security is best sought in home and family, not in status and possessions.

I have come home to hear these women again. I have returned to receive from the wells of their inspiration and the ever-flowing springs of their wisdom. My people are not saints. Like all of us, they are human. What they shared with me, what I learned from them, will be most life affirming when it swings wide the gate to the fountains of wisdom each of us has within.

Women, Barn Raisings, and Being There

It will never rain roses: when we want
To have more roses we must plant trees.
—GEORGE ELIOT,
The Spanish Gypsy (1868)

 elp your neighbor: This is the heart and soul of the Amish way. Nowhere is this more open for inspection or more vividly illustrated than in their barnraising tradition. My people prefer not to carry commercial insurance because they believe so firmly in being there for each other in times of need and crisis. Writers and interpreters call it mutual aid. My people call it "putting feet on your prayers."

They are seldom idle after catastrophe strikes. When a barn burns, they come with shovels and wheelbarrows to clean up. When a tornado hits, they come with hammers and nails to put things back together. When a friend struggles with depression, they come with buckets and mops to clean her house.

"You can't just sit and pray for people. You have to go help them." This belief in action so permeates Amish society that one day's grief and loss becomes the next day's rebuilding and romance. Rows of black-garbed men with yellow straw hats perched across the rafters of a new barn have intrigued photographers for generations. Women, carrying iced tea, coffee, and food, empathize with each other about lost treasure. By day's end, the shell of the barn has been restored, and carpenters go to work on the interior. Amish families who lose their barns to a fire often have fully functional new ones within several weeks. While these community building events are poetic and beautiful, they also symbolize a much larger story of shared burdens among my people.

Malinda tells me about a young Amish couple whose home was

destroyed in a fire. "They lost everything. Quilts and china. Wedding presents." She sighs, "But, you know, her aunts are getting together and making new quilts to replace the ones she lost. And the house is almost finished already." The hopeful inflection at the end of her last sentence demonstrates the value of being there for our neighbors and friends. "Putting feet on prayer" is not so much about helping strangers, although strangers, too, find themselves recipients of Amish aid, as it is about helping family members and friends.

Most of us cover our lives and possessions with insurance. We may not need volunteers to rebuild our houses, but we will always need others to stand beside us. We can make casseroles. We can shovel snow. We can paint porches. We can be there.

My friend Alonna has three small children and a next-door neighbor who loves to cook. "You know, lately she's been giving us something—a pot roast, a gallon of vegetable soup—almost every weekend. She claims they're leftovers, but I think she cooks with us in mind." It's a burden lifter for my friend, a busy working mother. It may not be as colorful as a barn raising, but its feet are just as strong and it is just as inspiring.

LOUISE STOLTZFUS

🌸 🌸

Volunteering the Amish Way

The nonprofessional volunteer world is a laboratory for self-realization.

—MADELEINE KUNIN,
Living a Political Life (1994)

Time is as valuable as money. More valuable sometimes. Time links woman to woman, woman to man, woman to child. Time conveys commitment. Time touches other souls in ways money never can. Time blesses both the giver and the receiver.

Amish women vividly illustrate their support for this theory by volunteering their time. "Helping others out," as my people call this integral part of their world, happens with a sort of natural smoothness and a surprising lack of coercion. Annie tells me, "People just jump in. They know what to do when someone needs help."

Everyone knows where to go and what to do when a barn burns, a hailstorm destroys a field of new corn, or a young mother falters under the pressure of her daily grind. The community's responses are often as easy and well orchestrated as going to church on Sunday morning. People gather to clean up and rebuild the barn. Neighboring farmers pitch in and plant the field again. Women move to the young mother's aid with mops, cleaning supplies, or childcare. "We do this because tomorrow we may be the ones needing help. What's more, it makes us feel good." These are the words most Amish women use to describe their service-driven society.

LOUISE STOLTZFUS

❧ ❧

We live in an era of changing governmental structures and deep cuts to social programs. Soup kitchens and shelters need volunteers because they no longer have funds to pay support staff. Schools and hospitals need help, especially in some of the poorest communities, because funding has been decreased. Libraries, retirement centers, and churches can use our time. Our money, too. But, like the Amish women who work so hard to lift each other's burdens, let us never underestimate the value of time.

Volunteering our time? It's a question of large enough import on the American stage to attract the attention of people like Colin Powell and of presidential summits. Many of us hope the call to volunteering will lead to significant changes in the American landscape, reengineering our communities and reconnecting us to the heart and core of neighborhood life. We can only hope the fanfare of large-scale programs does not detract us from the more immediate and manageable needs. Like women among my people, we will often be most blessed when we find quiet, neighborly ways to donate an ongoing supply of time and energy.

Working mothers who faithfully show up for one hour a week at their children's schools lend as much to the success of the volunteer movement as a countywide support program or a major relief agency.

So does the woman who bakes a cake for her neighbor. Or the teen-ager who paints a fence for an elderly friend. Or the child who learns about volunteering by serving food with his or her parents at a rescue mission on Thanksgiving Day. These ordinary places are where the rubber hits the road, where the buggy wheels stir up the gravel.

In Pursuit of Honest Pleasure

All the sky, to every point of the compass, became a soft blue and the clouds were white powder, so that in the end it was tenderness that triumphed. I went home to sound, cool sleep.

—Marjorie Kinnan Rawlings,
Cross Creek (1942)

To be whole and happy, most of us need more honest pleasure in our lives. Amish women know about pleasure. But my people often describe happiness and having a good time with words and scenes very different from those we might consider or choose.

"I love to sit on the deck behind our house and watch the sunset."

"At least once a week during the summer, my grandchildren walk over here because they know I'll probably have some fresh baked sweet rolls. That is so much fun, especially when their mother has time to come with them."

"What I like most about my life are my friendships with other women. We have the best times sitting together and visiting. We don't talk about world-shattering things, just the small, intimate details of our lives."

I am most intrigued by their inclination for taking pleasure in the everyday events of life. Women among my people tell of taking time to enjoy a baby's first smile and first steps. To compose a letter to a friend, have tea with a neighbor, or call on a sister. To sew a few stitches in a quilt, talk a few hours with a daughter, or sit a few minutes in the summer afternoon shade with a husband. They find the idea that pleasure might be reserved for weekends and vacations quite outside the context of their experience.

Friday night movies. Hotel weekend getaways. Vacations to the mountains, the seashore, or the lake. Few of these typical American pleasures appeal to Amish women. When they take vacations, they often structure the time around visits to friends and relatives in other Amish communities. Along the way, perhaps, they find time for a bit of sight-seeing. Which is why we may be surprised to discover an Amish family enjoying a beach on the Gulf Coast, a hike in the Appalachians, or a vista overlooking Yosemite National Park. Most Amish women find nothing inconsistent about mingling with the world in these public places, for they are discovering "God's great outdoors," as they often say to each other when reporting on such a trip.

To them pleasure is not about escape, it is about pleasantness and togetherness. Togetherness with God and friends and family. My people do not imagine pleasure to be synonymous with escape. Honest pleasure touches a place much deeper in the soul, where the spirit finds peace and hope is revived, where the body finds rest and life is sustained. Such peace and rest, such revival and sustenance, comes to each of us in many different ways. A good book on a long, winter evening. The sensation of yeast dough between the fingers. The warm and direct eyes and hands of a lover or dear friend. So it is that most Amish women are abundantly willing to forego weekend getaways and expensive vacations. To them the trade-offs are obvious—more time and money for the pursuit of honest pleasure.

Make no mistake, making time for pleasure sometimes requires sacrifice for Amish women as it does for us, the women of the world. It is no easier for most women among my people to set aside time for reading and resting than it is for most of us. The demands of their workaday world, too, are high. The house must be cleaned. The cows must be milked. The tomatoes must be canned. The children's school clothes will not sew themselves. But making time to feel good throughout the week is more important to most Amish women than desperately hanging on until the weekend brings its brief, elusive moment of escape.

It is a word of hope to all of us. The treadmill of demanding jobs and high-maintenance families holds so many in its endless, plodding grip. Evermore, it sometimes seems, our lives acquire more rigid schedules, with no time left for cappuccino with a friend or dinner with the family. Bosses and corporations take over. Deadlines and customers make their equal and sometimes opposite demands. Long hours draw themselves on our faces and hands, color our hair, and shadow our eyes.

The way of Amish women suggests that we stop the presses of such a life. That we perhaps choose to spend less money on escapism, which would require fewer hours of work and provide more time for the easels and palettes of genuine pleasure.

The Flowering
of Beauty

*Therefore, on every morrow, are we wreathing
A flowery band to bind us to the earth.*
—JOHN KEATS,
"A Thing of Beauty" (1818)

Many Amish women recognize, as we all do, that surrounding ourselves with beauty makes the world an easier place. Our living conditions directly affect not only physical comfort but also moods and emotional wellness. This, I think, is why my people often quickly transform the most humble and even dilapidated farmhouses into immaculately scrubbed homes filled with books, china, plants, and furniture.

Throughout the spring and early summer, they flock to local nurseries and garden outlets, often purchasing dozens of flats filled with plants of every description common to their part of the country. They go home to till the soil and cultivate luxurious beds of flowering plants, vegetables, and fruits. Colorful, weed-free arrangements of impatiens and marigolds, lilies and roses, ferns and gladioli envelop their houses, barns, and outbuildings. Immense gardens, often carved from the corner of a field, sprout leaf lettuce, radishes, and spring onions soon to be joined by the tiny shoots of peas, corn, and beans. On many Amish homesteads, every plot of soil, no matter how small, gives life to some useful plant. Useful either as a source of physical or spiritual nourishment.

Whether we live in sky-high condominiums, inner-city rowhouses, or suburban wildernesses of concrete, asphalt, and endless green grass, we, too, can listen to the poet Keats and heed the Amish women who so unconsciously follow his words. "A thing of beauty is a joy forever: / Its loveliness increases; it will never / Pass into nothingness; but still will keep / A bower quiet for us, and a sleep / Full of sweet dreams, and health, and quiet breathing."

We, too, may have around us things of beauty. A few marigolds in a window box or tulip bulbs along the edges of a walkway. Living green vines for the insides of our homes. An occasional work of art from a local fair. An old piece of furniture from Grandma's attic. We, too, may fill our homes with sweet dreams and health, making them places where it is easier to breathe.

Like many women among my people, Sadie spares little expense or imagination in the way she coordinates flowers and plants. At the height of summer, her rock garden suggests a great abstract painting. "I see a plant and think to myself, 'Oh, that would be good to put beside the snapdragons this year.' I don't know. I guess it just comes to me." Spoken like the artist she is.

It is worth an entire late-summer Sunday afternoon of driving slowly through an Amish community just to see the many varieties of flowering plants that decorate the grounds surrounding my people and their homes. Do not invade their privacy, and they will ignore you. Do not drive into their farmyards and lanes, and they will think perhaps you are gathering ideas for your own gardens. Do not take obvious photographs, and they will consider you a good neighbor enjoying the bounty of country life.

A More Mellow
Measure of the Seasons

To stay in one place and watch the seasons come and go is tantamount to constant travel: one is traveling with the earth.

—MARGUERITE YOURCENAR,
With Open Eyes (1984)

No matter what part of the earth we call home, we share in the ebb and flow of the seasons. In the moderate climates, we celebrate spring with the arrival of crocuses, dogwood, and azalea; summer with abundant fruits; autumn with colorful trees; and winter with the brightness of snow. In the tropics, we celebrate with exotic blooms like bird-of-paradise, royal poinciana, and jacaranda; the welcome rains and heat of summer; and the drier, cooler breezes of winter. Everywhere, the measures in the music of the earth are directed by the seasons.

Women among my people attune themselves to these movements. They look forward to autumn and winter because they bring relief from the frantic pace of gardening, preserving, and caring for the earth. They eagerly await spring and summer because these are the seasons that promise warmer air and explosions of color across a barren landscape.

Winter, on the other hand, mellows the busyness and grind of the everyday for these rural, working women. They have time to read. Time to take a whole day off to go shopping. Time to visit with sisters and friends. They rest for a season, like the soil and earth around them, and look forward to the faster beat of spring and summer.

LOUISE STOLTZFUS

In vivid contrast to this steady view of the seasons, many of us gladly enlist technology to overcome the pulses of nature. Electric lights keep our homes brightly lit through the dark days of winter. Air conditioners and climate-controlled buildings remove us from the suffocating and stilling heat of summer. Central heating units deliver us from the bone-numbing and quieting cold of winter. In our rush to control the climate of our cars, homes, and offices, we forget that we are also giving up the fine and best excuse for not working: "It's too hot (or too cold)."

We deprive ourselves of the very important slowing or quickening of each new season when we attempt to control the environment. The race from tightly closed homes to Freon-cooled cars to climate-controlled offices divorces us from a great deal more than heat and cold. It separates us from nature, from the molecules and pores of air and freedom, from the organic order that controls busyness. We are often left with sagging bodies and worried minds. Minds and bodies we describe with words and phrases such as "stress" or "burnout" and "I'm too busy" or "I feel tired all the time."

Let's make peace with the earth. Walk or bike to work when we can. Turn off the home air conditioners sometimes. Open the windows. Give in to the seasons.

Let's forget about controlling the climate. It is not possible, and it only adds extra strain to already overloaded psyches. That is not to say we should not complain about heat and cold. Perhaps it is complaining that makes the whims of weather and the movement of the seasons easier to take.

Dodgers Fans and Amish Roller Bladers

Let your moderation be known unto all.
—Book of the Philippians

The sight of a young Amish woman roller-blading along a two-lane rural highway catches many visitors by surprise. The incongruity of these simple, supposedly reserved women roller-blading in their plain dresses and aprons suggests a breakdown in the sensory neurons of the brain. "Surely we did not see what we just saw!" Roller bladers in Central

Park, yes. Roller bladers in swimsuits, weaving among the cars on Ocean Drive in South Beach, yes. Roller bladers along Lake Michigan, yes. But an Amish woman roller-blading along a country road? Well, maybe.

Like many of us, Amish women have a gentle love-hate relationship with sports. Young women play volleyball with the best of them, ice-skate on farm ponds in the wintertime, and, yes, they have been known to strap on a set of in-line skates for a quick spin to the village store or an early evening visit with the neighbors. They play a decent game of softball and sometimes run like the wind, long dresses flapping between their knees. When they marry, their youthful strength turns quickly to childbearing, the daily demands of motherhood, and running a household. They are not unlike many of us. They have little energy left for active participation in sports.

Rachel observes, "I guess you could say we leave the follies of our youth behind."

My paternal grandmother loved to say, "Everything in moderation; nothing to excess." She applied this to all of life, especially to playing games. She disliked the notion of any of us becoming obsessed with sports. Participation provided a healthy release for emotional tension and kept us physically fit. She may not have thought through the differences between spectator sports and active participation, but she understood obsession. She supported the Amish philosophy of no involvement in professional sports and consistently intoned her kind warning, "Everything in moderation."

For good reason, she thought. I grew up in an Amish family with a passion for sports. Baseball. Two-hand touch football. Volleyball. Ice-skating on neighborhood creeks and ponds. My brothers and I developed a streak of competitiveness that my grandmother, parents, and eventually the in-laws spent years trying to understand and curb.

We live in an East Coast Amish community but have always been die-hard Dodgers fans, thanks to my father's fascination with a Brooklyn Dodgers farm team that once called a field just outside Lancaster, Pennsylvania, its home park. The move from Brooklyn to Los Angeles did not deter him or us from rooting for the likes of Jackie Robinson, Sandy Koufax, and Don Drysdale. We followed their every move in the daily newspaper and occasionally watched parts of the World Series on a neighbor's television set or at the corner drugstore.

We were not an anomaly in the Amish community. Many Amish families enjoy sports, but most, thanks to people like my grandmother, have a clear sense of when enough is enough. They prefer controlled participation to spectator sports. They believe in staying physically fit, but they constantly remind each other that the excesses of profession-alism are not something they wish to support. It is easier for the women than the men, but the men, too, hear the same grandmotherly warnings and the same community guidelines against visiting nearby professional parks.

In a world of Friday night football, multimillion-dollar sports extravaganzas, and the exploitation of younger and younger stars, the advice of my Amish grandmother makes increasing sense. Physical fitness is one thing; an obsession with the bright lights of someone else's success is quite another. The one in moderation offers wellness; the other, because of its excesses, often proves my grandmother right. I am certainly richer for her admonitions. So are my brothers!

Amish Feminism

An indigenous feminism has been present in every
culture in the world and every period of history since
the suppression of women began.
—ROBIN MORGAN,
Sisterhood Is Global (1984)

*N*o, they are not feminists, the women who raised me.
There's not a single Gloria Steinem or Patricia Schroe-
der among them. They do not wish to align themselves
with any of the causes of the feminist movement, and
many are offended at the very thought.

That is, until they start talking about the nature of relationships between women and men in their society. Women have as important a role in Amish life as men. Women are not, nor should they allow themselves to become, doormats. Women deserve to be treated with complete consideration and genuine love by men. My people may laugh softly with anyone who points out the obvious feminism behind these principles, but they will hasten to repeat, "I am not a feminist."

I think perhaps they mean to say, as do many women who ride the "I am not" wagon train, that they have no time for the militance of those engaged in the struggle to influence policy making—of those whose voices sometimes become very strident in order to be heard. I think many women among my people are benevolent feminists.

These are women who are decisive about their personal worth, determined to realize their full potential, and delighted when they find partners and friends who help them do so. But they are also women who avoid the corridors of power, who have no desire to debate the questions of deep-seated discrimination of women, and who believe real change happens in the home, in the ways we teach our sons to treat women and our daughters to respond to men. And on that note, I think many Amish women are classic feminists.

Sons and daughters are raised in an atmosphere of fairness and equal opportunity. If the boys get to go swimming in the pond, so do the girls. If the girls have chores, so do the boys. If the young women are available to help make hay, they are called upon. If the young men are available to help get the house ready for a special event such as a wedding or church service, they are called upon. The typical division of labor around men's and women's work does exist, but many Amish households exhibit far less austerity on this matter than other religious and similarly inclined, middle-class American families. Girls are as important to the continuing growth and solid foundations of the Amish way as are boys.

On one level, this fairness issue is about a high regard for the task of mothering children. On another level, it is about common sense and treating each other well. Throughout Amish history, my people have nurtured women who choose not to become mothers with the same care they extend to those who do so.

When Lydia moved into her thirties with no marriage plans or prospects, her parents came to her with a generous proposal. They were ready to retire from the family farm. They would help her finance a house, putting the deed in her name. They would live on one side, she would live on the other in a private apartment. Her parents have died, and Lydia lives with gracious ease in her now paid-for home. Her story is repeated over and over among Amish single women.

My people live in a society that strives to treat women with consideration and reverence. Many Amish women believe this happens because they know how to stay in their places and because they don't kick over the traces in the way of many active feminists.

I think it has much more to do with expecting the men in their lives to treat them as partners, to treat them as persons with equal intelligence and insight, equal perseverance and pluck. I think it has much more to do with teaching their sons to act respectfully toward women and their daughters to act courteously toward men.

Freedom with Responsibility

*N*othing strengthens the judgment and quickens the conscience like individual responsibility.
—ELIZABETH CADY STANTON,
"The Solitude of Self" (1892)

*O*ne of my dad's favorite admonitions to his children was a two-word phrase, "Be responsible." This applied to everything from getting to work on time to avoiding the temptations of drugs, alcohol, tobacco, and sexual promiscuity. If you acted responsibly, you would not do anything to hurt yourself or another person. You could then be trusted with greater freedom. If you used your freedom well, you were a wise person.

Like many Amish, my parents believed freedom and responsibility went hand in hand, and they made direct connections between responsible behavior and free living. We were taught, first of all, to pick up our own toys and clothing, to sit quietly in church, to act respectfully toward each other, and to be thankful for small gifts such as a piece of candy or a pair of new shoes.

Demonstrations of responsibility were usually rewarded with increased freedom. When we sat still through a church service, we were trusted to sit with a favorite aunt (who might have pockets full of candy) the next time. When we picked up our toys, we were treated to an extra story at bedtime. When we acted with respect, we could perhaps go fishing or swimming, walk through the meadows to visit grandparents, or sit in the shade with a book through a long, hot summer afternoon.

My parents bought us few material things (they couldn't afford to), but they managed to pass on the advantages and gifts of responsible living. These included a respect for authority, an intuition about the limits of power and influence, and the sure knowledge that freedom also reflected accountability.

Amish women believe these advantages and gifts, when transferred faithfully to children, will bear fruit for a lifetime. Young people who internalize these simple truths will think twice before joining in the sometimes irresponsible actions common to the culture of youth. They may not always be able to control temptation, but they will have learned the waste and loss of squandering their youthful energies on careless actions and thoughtless words.

Young people of any culture, raised in an atmosphere of shared freedom seldom become exactly who their parents imagined or hoped, but no matter where they go or who they become, they never forget the valuable lessons learned from their upbringing—which is the best possible reason for all of us to trust our young people with responsibility and freedom.

The freedom part of the equation is more difficult for many parents, but it cannot be separated from simplicity, from letting go. When we let go, we simplify our own lives. When we are able to trust our children to express free will within the context of responsible living, we will have discovered a less stressful way to see children through their youth into the commitments and pleasures that define adult experiences and understandings.

In Search
of Utopia

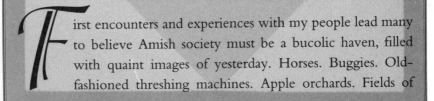

Yet I confess there are many things in the Commonwealth of Utopia which I wish our own country would imitate—though I don't really expect it will.
—SIR THOMAS MORE,
Utopia (1516)

First encounters and experiences with my people lead many to believe Amish society must be a bucolic haven, filled with quaint images of yesterday. Horses. Buggies. Old-fashioned threshing machines. Apple orchards. Fields of corn. Windmills and waterwheels. Soft-spoken people. Women who give all their lives to caring for children and making a home. Men who labor from dawn till dusk behind horse-drawn farm equipment, raising crops and feeding their families. Children who are well loved and well fed, energetic but calm, contented and at peace with themselves and their world. When life is good, as it is for many of my people, this picture comes very close to reality.

But there is also a dark side. There are broken homes, sad children, and authoritarian leaders. There is sometimes evidence of the division and disappointment common to many ingrown, tightly woven societies. Life among my people is not always good. Those who learn to know the Amish soon experience both the good and bad. Sometimes the darkness seems too much; sometimes the brightness seems surreal.

I worked for many years at an educational and interpretive center on Amish life. We received many inquiries about joining the Amish. How did it work? Was it possible? How soon could we make the arrangements?

We could only point these searchers to sympathetic people among the Amish, to those who were willing and able to say, "Yes, it is possible to join our community. No, it is not easy. To become an

Amish person, you must go all the way. You must live Amish, dress Amish, and think Amish."

Although it is relatively easy to live and dress like my people, most seekers find it difficult, and even impossible, to think like the Amish, which is why I have always wondered about the wisdom of searching for utopia in another person's experience. Those of us who are intent on finding answers to our problems by separating ourselves from our own stories, by joining the Amish, for example, will probably be disappointed. My people are human. They make mistakes. They know how difficult it will be to transfer visions of horses and buggies, fields of corn, and quiet children to the harder principles of a faithful Amish life. The Amish way also requires sacrifice, obedience, and submission.

My people are certain that women of the world will never find utopia in the Amish community. Rather, most Amish women would recommend that each of us rely on the innate beauty and strength of our personal story. That each of us learn to trust the inner light connecting us to the women and people, the spirit and peace, of our own way.

About her encounter with the Amish way, the artist Sue Bender writes, "I had hoped that if I could learn the secret of the Amish life of 'no frills,' it would help me make great art. But their secret is there aren't any secrets." None of us could say it better.

The Amish women I know want all of us to remember this truth whenever we are tempted to leap out of our world into theirs. My people believe that the best way to engage the mystery of life, to solve our problems, is to go within, to uncover and articulate our own narrative.

No Excuses for Shunning

We hand folks over to God's mercy, and show none ourselves.

—GEORGE ELIOT,
Adam Bede (1859)

Shunning. Many of us have wondered how shunning fits into the Amish story. What does it mean? How do these otherwise gentle, pastoral people justify what, at its best, sounds like pushing people away and, at its worst, raises the question of abuse? What do my people mean when they speak of "having nothing to do" with former members of their congregations?

My paternal grandmother agonized over this question most of her life. She thought *der Bann* (the ban or shunning) exacted much too high a price. Although she kept her promises to her community, she never agreed with strict shunning and dedicated her life to treating those who left the Amish faith, including some of her children, with respect and care. She was not unusual

Most women and men among my people believe shunning preserves congregational integrity, but they also understand how dark it turns when driven by personality differences and power. They practice and preach reason and sound judgment, yielding to the letter of the law while keeping their hearts and homes open to family members and friends who leave.

Like my grandmother, they make no excuses for those among them who use this doctrine to hurt or punish people who may need nothing more than love and forgiveness. But they also find it very difficult to explain what often appears to be "a secret side of the Amish community." In their eyes, it is not secret. Within the community, it is a much talked about, complex problem.

A daughter runs away from her abusive mother and is shunned for leaving. A family disagrees with congregational leaders, igniting a personality dispute that threatens the power structure. The family is excommunicated when it becomes impossible for them to stay. A businesswoman refuses to sell goods to a customer who was once Amish because of overzealous interpretations of scriptures such as the admonition "Have no company with them." These are the distressing and regrettable stories, and they happen because my people are human. Amish women, like my grandmother, seldom try to justify such extreme behavior. They only bow their heads and say, "Sometimes we are wrong."

When I was seventeen years old, my parents left the Old Order Amish church and joined a more moderate group called the Beachy (the surname of an early leader) Amish. Promptly, they were excommunicated and placed in the ban by their former congregation. Aside from my grandmother's sadness, the only disruptions in our extended family life grew out of the need to satisfy the letter of the law. The injunctions "Do not eat with them" and "Have no company with them" were modified to setting up separate tables, often in the same room. Although our moderately different lives sometimes mystified this extraordinary woman, we received not one ounce less love and care. She was a compassionate and thoughtful person who taught us that nothing is ever what it seems. So it is with the Amish and shunning.

Rather than reacting with disbelief and disappointment in the presence of imperfection, we might all do well to breathe deeply and examine the darknesses in our own belief systems. How are we closing the doors to relationships? How are we keeping others from experiencing the light and freedom of forgiveness? When we discover darkness, we could not do better than to bow our heads and say, "Sometimes we are wrong."

The Link between Criticism and Humility

Cracked things often hold out as long as whole things; one takes so much better care of them!
—JANE WELSH CARLYLE,
letter (1857)

My people have a refreshing perspective on negative criticism. They say it's good for the soul. They say it keeps them honest. They say it protects them from pride. I have been close to Amish women who found criticism hard to take, but I have been continually confounded by their ability to pull back from the sting and ask, "What can I learn from this?"

"What can we learn from this?" That is the classic Amish response to unflattering portrayals of their lives. When a major television show calls them abusive and secretive, when a national newspaper accuses them of damning and disowning those who leave, they do their best to understand how their complex story could take such a disturbing turn in the hands of an interpreter. They seldom hide their heads in the sand. Some write letters after the fact, attempting to explain the intricate interweavings of their society. Many simply say, "We must do better."

My people know that criticism is sometimes justified. That mistakes and imperfections hurt other people. That indiscretions and lack of control interrupt peaceful coexistence. That all of us must learn to accept censure and disapproval. That we must also learn to say, "I am wrong" and "I am sorry." For the soul is diminished without introspection.

Our responses to criticism, whether justified or unjustified, shape the world we create. As we open ourselves to other interpretations of our lives, we broaden the laws and rules that codify our existence. We are enlightened. We may react with anger, laughter, tears, acceptance, or all of these emotions at once, but we cannot turn into ostriches. For passion shines a light on the soul, and standing, face lifted to its rays, keeps us humble.

Several years ago, *The Philadelphia Inquirer* published a very unflattering piece in its Sunday magazine on shunning and its applications in the Amish community. Overlaid across a photograph of an Amish woman's head covering was the title, a single word in bright red print, "Damned." I knew the family interviewed by the writer and found myself responding to this unsympathetic view of my people with anger and frustration. The picture painted was one of confusion and loss, of nonsensical rules and threatening communications. Of preachers who would not listen. Of parents, brothers, and sisters who could not understand. Of an uncompromising, dictatorial faith.

In my view, the writer had inaccurately positioned a narrow part of the Amish story, a divisive practice within the church, as the single defining element of my people and their culture. Several weeks later, I visited Mary and David, friends of the family profiled in the article. I told them of my feelings.

David looked at me and said, "Well, we need those kinds of stories. We sometimes have too much touristy fluff, making us out to be much better than we are. That kind of criticism just keeps us humble." I have not forgotten David's words. I can only hope to become more like him.

A Leitmotif of Pride

The best of all friends is pride.
—GERTRUDE ATHERTON,
Julia France and Her Times (1912)

Though it will, no doubt, take a lifetime to come to terms with either of these virtues, I am grateful for every lesson in humility and pride gleaned from my Amish childhood and early years. The leitmotif "Pride goeth before a fall" anchors me to the teachings of my youth, as does its opposite theme,

"False humility is a form of pride." Within each of us, the yearning for harmony seldom reaches the stage without some accompaniment of remembered lessons from our homes. As the score moves toward life's climax, the balance between humility and pride begins to look, feel, and sound as seamless as a great operatic performance. Such was the case with my paternal grandparents.

I am blessed by their legacy of true humility and honest pride. They lived in an immensely beautiful, early-eighteenth-century American manor house. A centerpiece of the rural neighborhood, it was the envy of all my friends. Even today, these people tell me stories of visiting my grandparents and "sliding down the grand stair rail" or discovering some fascinating crevice in the home's much admired attic or basement. My own memories of the house and its surroundings cannot be separated from the people whose presence bathed every room in warmth and eloquent expressions of the good life.

I remember my grandmother's patience as we joined her to prepare meals, bake cookies, plant gardens, or preserve fruits and vegetables. She thought mistakes just made everything better the next time. I remember my grandfather's quiet pride in the rows of As and Bs on our report cards. He wanted us to be successful. I remember sobbing in sorrow when evening came and it seemed too soon to leave the circle of their care. They were proud people who surrounded their grandchildren with a sense of personal dignity and self-worth, teaching us to delight in our own and others' accomplishments and achievements. They were also humble Amish people constantly reminding themselves and those around them of the precarious balance between hubris and healthy pride, between false humility and a humble spirit. Their words were in tune with one of the great themes of the Amish way, "We must be humble, but we must never take pride in our humility."

In the broad spaces beyond the Amish experience, many of us struggle for this same balance. We take pleasure in triumph and success, but we also recognize the agony of pride gone awry, yielding as it so often does to the corrupting power that destroys families, communities, and nations. My people call this "the sin of pride." It is this sin they try so diligently to avoid when they say, "We must be careful not to become proud." Sometimes they succeed, sometimes they do not.

Learning the recitative between humility and pride requires a lifetime of practice and performance. The presentation is never perfect, but it is always affecting. It is never above criticism, but it is always civilizing. It is never only about the performers; it is always also about the audience.

The Comfort of Language

Our native language is like a second skin.
—CASEY MILLER AND KATE SWIFT,
The Handbook of Nonsexist Writing (1980)

Many of us have a comfort language, a language that joins us to our family and home. Long Islanders have their accent. So do southerners. And Minnesotans. Recent immigrants speak Spanish, Vietnamese, or Korean within the shelter of their homes. The distinctive English dialect of the African American community warms the soul at extended family gatherings and Sunday afternoon dinners.

For my people, the language that soothes is *Deitsch* (also called Pennsylvania Dutch). It is a comfortable German dialect with roots in the Black Forest region of southern Germany, and its intonations and words help to preserve the differences that distinguish Amish society. *Deitsch* (pronounced with a long *i*) is spoken at home and is not a written language.

Many Amish children use it exclusively until they are four or five years old, often speaking little English until the last year before they enter first grade. Teachers learn to compensate for those whose first day of school may be more intimidating because of a new language.

In the 1970s, I taught for three terms in a one-room Amish school just outside the tiny village of White Horse, Pennsylvania. Of the twenty-some first graders who started school in those years, I had only one six-year-old who could not speak English on her first day. I enjoyed giving instructions in English and following them with a *Deitsch* interpretation, for it gave me a chance to practice a dialect I had already started using less and less.

Four weeks into the term, young Mary came to me one morning

and proudly announced, "Teacher, you don't have to tell me the directions in *Deitsch* anymore." I was a little sad to oblige but delighted to know this child would always have a firm foundation in her family's comfort language.

Like many Americans whose mother tongue is not English, my people understand the importance of learning the official language. For Amish women, English is the language of business and commerce, the language they use for all written communication, including cards and letters to each other. Generally, they speak it well, with only a trace of the dutchified accent common to some parts of eastern Pennsylvania. Almost without exception, though, they favor the comfort and familiarity of *Deitsch* in their interactions with each other.

Our comfort languages and accents lend us communication skills we might all strive to remember. As we seek ways to mainstream ourselves, to avoid becoming the subjects of stares and questions, let us not forget the particular flavors that hold us to the cultures and languages of our forebears. When we manage to sustain the memories of *fastnachts*, half-moon pies, and *Deitsch*; of jambalaya, mint juleps, and Cajun; of southern fried chicken, turnip greens, and Ebonics; of rice, beans, and Spanish, we save more than food and language. We save the distinguishing features that mark our view of the world. We save words no other languages can express and flavors no other foods can produce.

My people know this. I know it, but still I have gone the way of the world. That is the story of the great American mosaic and melting pot. In our rush to be similar, let us not forget to absorb the good in our past. To bathe in the familiar aromas and sounds of the people who gave us life. Perhaps, we will find they wear as well as soft cotton dresses, wrapping us in the tranquil touch of old homes and good times and renewing our energies for the more rapid pace of similarity and sameness.

Amish Women and Good Gossip

Gossip is theology translated into experience.
—KATHLEEN NORRIS,
Dakota (1993)

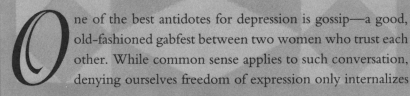

One of the best antidotes for depression is gossip—a good, old-fashioned gabfest between two women who trust each other. While common sense applies to such conversation, denying ourselves freedom of expression only internalizes our pains and poisons. I am sometimes dismayed by the irrational fear many women have of gossip.

Some religious communities adopt the premise that gossip is inherently evil. They are right that repeating idle talk and rumors about the private affairs of others is often unwise. They are not right when they declare many forms of communication among women gossip and call us sinners when we pour out our frustrations and hurts to our sisters, families, and friends.

Influences from these belief systems continually creep around the edges of Amish society. Women among my people occasionally cite fear of gossip as a reason for not permitting telephones inside their homes. Easy access, it is said, encourages idle conversation and wastes time. Women, for reasons not necessarily plausible, are believed to be more susceptible to these charms than men—a suggestion openly questioned and debated by many Amish women. Few believe they have more problems with gossip than the men in their lives. "I don't want a telephone inside because I think my husband would use it more often than I would!" is an exclamation I've heard more than once.

Much of the goodness and strength of my people rests on the ability of most Amish women to overcome objections to gossip and to participate in open communication. From light chatter over quilts to heavy discussions at family get-togethers, the tightly gathered Amish community depends on this intimate sharing of information to sustain itself. Good gossip is a friend. It relieves stress. It sends many a woman home to her family refreshed and invigorated. Refreshed because she has given voice to her fears and concerns. Invigorated because she has received comfort and encouragement from her peers.

Even so, the Amish church patriarchy still occasionally speaks against "the evils of gossip." Many of the women I know couch their words in careful language: "I just want you to know that I'm not gossiping. I'm telling you this so you will pray for me [or join me in praying for someone else]."

Whenever I'm with an Amish woman who gives voice to her burdens with such words, I am tempted to shout "Bravo!" Another woman has chosen to lean on the long history my people have for mutual support and care. She has found a way to share her concerns while still holding to the principles of her faith. She has not been intimidated by patriarchal interpretations that ask her to remain silent and apart from another's strength. She has found rest on the solid foundations of the Amish experience.

I find few societal problems more sad than patriarchal systems gone bad. These systems, many without the checks and balances of the Amish patriarchy, are everywhere among us. When it's not a church structure demanding obedience, it's a husband or father or employer. Whenever and wherever we meet women who exhibit an unwillingness to speak their concerns and problems to other women, we need to consider the ways of Amish women. We need to encourage more conversation, rather than less. Emotional distress, and even painful secrets, often lie behind the hesitation to speak.

Perhaps we can help each other overcome uncertainties about gossip by stating clearly, as my people often do, the differences between idle gossip and what we might call the energy of good gossip and prayer. Good gossip fixes its sight on thoughtful communication. It allows us to express our frustrations and fears. It releases the debilitating stress and tension of feeling alone, of feeling that no one understands. When we gossip, we find that other women (and men) share our concerns, identify with our pain and pleasure, and join in the hope that talking and praying will alleviate depression and sorrow.

Speak Well
of Others

Allowing yourself to be a subject of gossip is one of the sacrifices you make, living in a small town. And the pain caused by the loose talk of ignorant people is undeniable.

—KATHLEEN NORRIS,
Dakota (1993)

*T*here also exists a form of gossip that is definitely not useful. It is that malicious tearing down of another person's life and ideas that reveals much more about the person gossiping than the subject of the gossip. Men are as likely to do this as women. Malicious gossip is not gender specific, it's about power. And the desire for power haunts all of us.

The women who raised me tried to pass on the differences between good and bad gossip. They loved to talk—about ideas, the weather, philosophies, their gardens, and people. Perhaps most of all about people, because talking about others helped them to understand themselves. A story about someone else's great good fortune inspired them to work harder. A story about someone else's misfortune reminded them they were not the only people to whom bad things happened.

In their communion, in their conversations, they aimed to speak well of others. They recognized that all of us are shadowed by both good and bad. By sadness but also by joy. By an abundance of common sense and kindness but also sometimes by an astonishing lack of either.

So they told their stories and said, "Always speak kindly of others" and "If you can't say something good, don't say anything." Don't say anything was a pretty high ideal, but the principle often helped stop an out-of-control train of words, as they reminded each other that, indeed, there must also be something good that could be said.

I'll never forget one such life lesson in gossip. My brothers and I were gathered around the kitchen table doing homework. I was feeling especially aggrieved about receiving what I thought was unfair treatment related to some dispute that I have long since forgotten. My mother stood nearby, pressing dresses and shirts, her ironing board facing the table where we were working. She listened to my long list of childish complaints about my brothers and their behavior—behavior she probably didn't know about.

When I was finished, she ignored their protestations, asked them to leave the room, and calmly explained that my outburst only proved that I was no better than they were. I disagreed vehemently, but she stuck to her position. And that's where she left it, instructing me to finish my homework. If she had scolded my brothers because of my grievances, the scene in that kitchen would have been very different.

But my mother very wisely chose another way. She took the time to hear me out, she refrained from using my complaints to discipline my brothers, and she pointed out my motives. It was a good and wise lesson I have remembered many times in the years since that rather dramatic kitchen performance. Thanks to my mother, I also have a much stronger basis for self-examination.

The challenges of balancing the good and the bad never leave us. We reach for the ideal and then fall far short. But we cannot let mistakes keep us from trying, for only as we achieve understanding will we grow. Only as we are guided by self-awareness and parents who care will we find security and safety. May we all be as wise as my mother, with our children and with each other.

The Echoes of Their Voices

Choice is the essence of what I believe it is to be human.

> —LIV ULLMANN,
> *Choices (1984)*

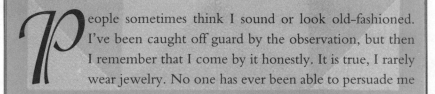

People sometimes think I sound or look old-fashioned. I've been caught off guard by the observation, but then I remember that I come by it honestly. It is true, I rarely wear jewelry. No one has ever been able to persuade me to pierce my ears, though a few of my friends have tried. I understand, but still I ask, "Why do you feel sorry for me because I don't want to poke holes in my ears? Why do you feel sorry for me because I don't have or want 'little doohickeys' to stick in the holes?" There it is: an echo of my maternal grandmother's old-fashioned voice.

Some years ago I spent a weekend in New York with a friend. He pointed out that he felt safer walking the streets with me because I wasn't wearing jewelry. Aha! Now there's a reason, I told him, not to wear jewelry. The truth, as he suspected, is much more complex. I seldom wear jewelry because of the old-fashioned women who taught me how to live and think and dress.

We came home to Lancaster, and he soon went back to dating women with jewelry. "Well, if the jewelry was all he cared about, you're definitely better off without him." There it is: the echo of my mother's voice.

Sometimes, when I tune in to these women and their voices, I'm surprised by how much the echoes have influenced my life. I wonder whether I should update my persona. A few of my friends, very kindly of course, have suggested that I begin with my accent, which imitates the flat *a*s and *o*s of my Amish foreparents.

For example, I was once having dinner at a crowded counter in a tiny Chinese restaurant in San Francisco. Two sentences into a conversation with the person next to me, he asked, "Were you ever Amish?" *Do I look Amish?* I thought to myself. To him I acknowledged my lineage. "I could tell by the way you talk," he said. "I used to live in Lancaster County."

Maybe I'll take speech lessons. Maybe I'll color my hair. Maybe I'll even pierce my ears. But, then again, maybe I won't. I like the way I am. I like my gray hair, my smooth earlobes, and my manner of speech. I like it that halfway around the world people can sometimes tell where I come from. And I love going home to my mother's house, where I can hear the cadence and echoes of the voices that shaped my life.

Whatever the voices that have shaped our lives, may we find in them a bit of the old-fashioned meter and beauty that keeps us coming home. Though we move far from the people and stories that made us who and how we are, we can never completely shake the influences they have on our lives. Sometimes, it feels just as good to embrace them. To come away from the hustle and bustle of our lives and be soothed by the bouncing echoes of our mothers' and grandmothers' voices.

LOUISE STOLTZFUS

❧ ❧

Sound No Trumpets for My Giving

When you give to the needy, do not announce it with trumpets. Do not let your left hand know what your right hand is doing.

—JESUS,
Book of Matthew

*A*mish women take these words of Jesus quite literally. They give freely—of time and money—to those in need, but they sound no trumpets. They prefer anonymity. My people support various Mennonite-related relief agencies, arriving at the local headquarters of these organizations by the van- and busload to spend a day quilting, packaging food parcels, or sorting donated clothing. When they give money, it is with the conviction that those who seek reward for their generosity here on earth will, without doubt, forfeit reward in the life to come.

"Let not your left hand know what your right hand gives" is the chorus that follows most stanzas describing Amish giving practices. My brother is a public relations director for one of the Mennonite relief agencies. "I've had Amish come up to me, shake my hand, and pass large amounts of cash to me. They want no recognition." Both humility and sacrifice inform this interpretation of service. Whatever my people give—time or money—they try to give humbly and without expecting return. Whatever they do—service or sacrifice—they try to do kindly and without immediate reward.

Amish women make quilts and comforters. They bake breads, pies, cakes, and cookies. They coordinate auctions to sell these goods, raising money either for specific needs in their own community or for worldwide relief organizations. Whether they donate a morning of labor to a sick neighbor or several months' work to organize an auction, women like my friend Sadie give hundreds of hours a year to causes they believe in. "You know, with medical costs the way they are, young families often just cannot keep up when an accident or sickness happens. We might raise money with a pizza supper or chicken pot pie dinner. Or we'll have a quilt or country auction. We try to bear each other's burdens."

Bearing each other's burdens permeates Amish thought on the subject of giving and receiving. It is as important to receive graciously as to give graciously. When I was a child, my parents lost their farm during a severe financial crisis. As the roughest winter of their poverty spread its gloom, my mother despaired one evening when she had scarcely enough food for supper. Later that same week a large box of frozen meat appeared on our front porch. We never knew who put it there, but thanks to someone's anonymous generosity, we made it through the winter. We have never forgotten.

There is a freshness about this way of giving that attracts me. I am no longer Amish, though, and I often choose to be thanked. I cannot fathom making a gorgeous quilt and donating it to a relief auction anonymously. I like the trumpets too much. When I say these things to Rachel, she shakes her head and smiles, "I guess that's why you're not Amish."

Perhaps there is also a broader lesson in the Amish way, the lesson of watching out for our neighbors. Many American families live at the poverty line. Some hide it well behind suburban grass enclosures and common entrances to high-rises. Are we asking the right questions in our churches and places of work? Do we know when the person sitting next to us suffers? Do we take the opportunity to reach out? We may not be Amish, we may have no desire to emulate the Amish concept of service and sacrifice, but we can still give. Even when we receive few thank-yous and no reward.

Sewing for Our Grandmothers

Just feel the joy and liberation!
Become one with the fabric; feel its rhythms;
understand the medium!
Everything leads to freedom!
—NANCY CROW,
Improvisational Quilts (1995)

Many of the women I grew up with took great pleasure in sewing. They made their own clothing. They sewed for their husbands, daughters, and sons. They pieced quilts. They embroidered pillowcases, towels, and samplers. They loved fabric and sought out dry-goods stores as poets and novelists seek out bookstores. They had a passion for the simple joys of stitching.

My maternal grandmother was such a woman. I remember her best with her lap full of fabric, embroidery thread, and sewing notions, working diligently on what she called her handwork. For hours she would sit, softly pushing needle and thread through fabric, all the while commiserating about the world. Sometimes she spoke of peril and danger. Other times she spoke of hope and helpfulness. Whatever the moment's mood or lesson, she seemed to turn, without fail, to some telling proverb to make her point.

Her fondness for "Idle hands are the devil's workshop" never ceased to confuse me as I tried to decipher the connection between my hands, the devil, and a workshop. She had no time for analysis. To her the interpretation was simple. It meant her granddaughters would be wise to learn how to knit, crochet, embroider, and sew. If we kept our hands so occupied, we would have fewer distractions and easier lives. She wanted us to be like her.

Many Amish women are like my grandmother. They love to sew. The ebb and flow of needles and thread, fabric and sewing machines, keeps them close to the changing tides of their creative powers. They relax. Their sewing rooms are a refuge from the everyday routines of farm and country living.

Women who enjoy sewing, whether or not they are Amish, understand this almost spiritual connection with fabric and color. They tell of loving the smell and feel of fabric. Of gazing in awe at the beautiful clothing, blankets, and quilts their obsession with combining fabric and thread brings to their lives and homes.

While others of us read novels or turn to exercise regimens for release and relaxation, these women stitch and sew. Their creations are a testament to the ageless wonder of women's work, the indescribable joy of making something that will outlast us. My people resonate with anyone who has rekindled an interest in sewing. They rejoice when we, too, find comfort in this domestic art. Like my grandmother, they know our lives will be enriched when neither our hands nor imaginations lie idle.

Quiltings, a Lifeline for Women

Pieces of lives
Stitches and secrets
Pieces of women's lives.
—MOLLY NEWMAN
AND BARBARA
DAMASHEK,
Quilters (1986)

*S*outhern women call them bees. Midwesterners call them quilting bees. My people call them quiltings. For Amish women, the stories and tales shared at these gatherings are often as important and as rich as the fabrics, colors, and patterns of the quilts themselves. Double-wedding-ring designs reign over family tales of the marriage of Miriam's daughter or the birth of Sally's baby boy. Embroidered patches with birds of every description awaken memories of Grandma or Aunt Sarah. "Do you know what happened to Mother's center-diamond quilt?" or "Where were you when Mother told us about buying the farm?" someone asks. Someone else nearly always knows the answer and wants to tell the story.

There is nothing quite like an Amish quilting. Indeed, there is nothing quite like an all-day get-together with the women of any family, neighborhood, or community. Our mothers and grandmothers had time for these events. Do we? Too quickly, perhaps, we say no. The kids have soccer practice. The boss demands ten-hour days. A movie or dinner out will be more relaxing. Perhaps.

Then again? In the last twenty years, countless quilting groups have emerged from the ruins of urban and suburban isolation. Women from all levels of society have returned to stitching fabric and quilting because they like the companionship of other women. Because they find the gatherings restful, satisfying, and rewarding.

Local newspapers often print invitations to quilting guilds. Galleries, museums, and malls have quilt shows. In the busyness of running children to and fro, meeting deadlines, and cooking meals, we may wish to make time for ourselves, some fabric, and a needle and thread. Who knows? We may be surprised.

My mother is a quilter. So was her mother. So are all of her sisters. And most of her sisters-in-law. I do not begin to match their speed or skill with needles and thread, but I go to their quiltings to remember my grandmother, to learn from my mother's sisters, and to trade gossip with my cousins. I go because I hear portions of my mother's family story, portions I would know nothing about if I gave in to the little voice, "I'm just too busy." I go because I love the shapes and shadows of an old-fashioned quilting frame. I like sitting next to my mother somewhere around the edge of a quilt. I miss my grandmother and often find her again in the words of these women, her daughters and granddaughters.

The large, stretched quilt gradually disappears as it is rolled into the frame and toward the center. Energy builds to "get it out" before we have to go home. As late-afternoon light darkens the shadows, we novices yield our chairs to the experts. The final stitches meet in rapid flourishes of goodwill and pride in a task well done. We are women of a family who have found healing in an heirloom. Let us remember this when next we feel too busy to reconnect to a quilting bee or a family story.

Pacing Ourselves to Manage Stress

The bow always strung will not do.
—GEORGE ELIOT
Middlemarch (1871)

I sat in Lydia's kitchen one morning listening to her talk about stress. The quietness of her home, the loveliness of the fields outside her window, seemed in contradiction with everything I thought about stress. "Yes, I am sometimes much too busy." She has pressures of a kind most of us know nothing about.

Every week the house must be cleaned—top to bottom. The yard raked and mowed. Flower beds weeded. Fruits and vegetables planted and gathered. Dresses sewn. Meals prepared.

She runs a race with busyness almost every day of her life. So do we. Not with mops and cleaning rags, maybe, but with messages and calendars as we juggle family and work schedules. Not with rakes and hoes but with cars, telephones, and fax machines. Not with fabric and food but with job deadlines, customer requests, and good deeds.

There is so much more to life than work. Rest and friendship. Good books and close companions. A slow-moving stream. A mountain path. A city park and a picnic lunch. Lydia reflects on the challenges of managing her life so she can cherish these simple pleasures. "I have learned to pace myself."

She still gets her work done, she says. Not as often and not as quickly. Maybe she makes soup and salad for supper instead of a full-course, meat-and-potatoes meal. Maybe she doesn't finish a new dress in time for that special event and has to wear an old one. Maybe she passes up a chance to sell a quilt because she has no time to make it.

It's that thing runners and bikers do throughout a marathon to conserve energy for the final burst at the finish line. While keeping the pace, they deliberately refuse to overcommit. Without question, athletes who do this take a risk, losing more often than they win. But it's worth it because an even gait makes the difference between being a contender and dropping far behind. Or not even finishing the race.

It is one of life's more difficult disciplines. The moment we relax, one of those once-in-a-lifetime chances comes by. More satisfaction. More money. More influence. Sometimes we cannot let it pass, but to pace ourselves, we must let go of something else.

Several years ago, I said no to overwhelming pressures at work, which resulted in the loss of what was once a very good job. It was frightening beyond anything I expected, but it relieved a monumental stress load. I learned to live with less money and less satisfaction. And I never once regretted the decision or had any desire to return.

Learning to pace ourselves takes a lifetime of practice and commitment. We never achieve complete success because even as we resolve to say no, a continuing stream of opportunities move in and out of our field of vision. We must reach for some. We must pace ourselves to let others go.

Slowing Down

She moved with a slowness that was a sign of rich-
ness; cream does not pour quickly.
—REBECCA WEST,
Black Lamb and Grey Falcon (1941)

Slow down. That is what my people think the world needs to
do. The metaphors for slowness abound in the Amish community. Horses and buggies. The exquisite slow chant of
Sunday morning hymn singing. The labored chugging of an
old Maytag wringer washer. The ding, dinging of battery-operated

alarm clocks. Homes free of microwave ovens, telephones, televisions, and radios.

Many of my people even arrange their days around what they call "slow time." Translated, this means they don't change the clocks each spring and fall, staying the full year on standard time. They see no reason for more evening daylight hours. And as farmers they feel the switch troubles the animals, especially milk-producing cows. Women and men who own small businesses often change to daylight savings time in their shops but remain on slow time at home.

After my parents lost their farm in the late 1950s, my father went to work in a factory, and we began changing our clocks. It was a sign, my grandmother thought, that we were becoming more worldly, more entrenched in the rush and whirl of modernity. She may have been right.

We never went back to slow time. We traded in the buggy for a car. We sing much faster now, and some of us even have microwave ovens, televisions, and radios. Signs of the times: That's what my grandmother called the gadgetry of modern life. She'd say the phrase with a deep sigh and gratefully return to the slow motion of her life. These many years later, I sometimes find myself reaching back to that place, exhausted by the tempo and tedium of full-scale technology.

How can I slow down? That's what I ask myself. It seems to me that

LOUISE STOLTZFUS

❧ ❧

a willingness to live with less is the first step in this process. When we begin removing the influences of more, of immediacy and right now, from our lives, we may face some hard questions. Why do I eat out so often? Do we really need a microwave? Or a brand-new, large-screen television? Why do I work in a place that drains every bit of my energy?

As working mothers, we might resolve to ask for more flexible schedules. Maybe we give up a pay hike and cut back hours instead. Maybe we ask our husbands to do the same. Maybe we ask our children to consider public schools or fewer expensive outfits or life without Friday night trips to the mall.

As business owners, we might look for ways to run our companies more efficiently. Maybe we can live with less work and less money. Maybe we reach out to employees worn down by the tiresome pace of racing against deadlines. Maybe we work together to establish more reasonable daily timetables. Indeed, studies have shown that more evenly calibrated, parent-friendly workplaces often distinguish themselves with happier people and higher productivity.

Living with less? I think it's one of the great challenges of our day. I also think it is inextricably tied to employers and employees both asking difficult questions and making difficult resolutions. May we have the courage to slow down and try.

The Sanity of Evening

If there be one hour of the twenty-four which has the life of day without its labor, and the rest of night without its slumber, it is the lovely and languid hour of twilight.

—L. E. LANDON,
Francesca Carrara (1834)

*T*here should be in every day a time to stop. A time to wind down from the high energy and frantic movement of commerce and work. A time to sit quietly on a porch, patio, or park bench. A time to reflect and be still.

Amish women do this in the evening. They gather their children around them. Daughters and mothers put aside cooking and cleaning. Fathers and sons come in from the barns, fields, and shops. The uneven, frenzied pace of planting and harvesting, building and restoring, slowly yields to the more even pace of the setting sun and fading twilight. Everyone gradually comes to a stop around books, a cup of hot chocolate, a bowl of ice cream, or some watermelon. It's the best time of the day.

That was how it always seemed to me. We loved and looked forward to the evening. In the wintertime, we seldom worked after the six o'clock supper dishes were done. We read, played games, or lounged by the woodstove while Mom and Dad perused the newspaper and talked about their hopes and dreams. In the summer, we might have a garden to hoe or a lawn to mow. But as soon as we were done, everyone came together under the sprawling maple in the backyard and watched the sun go down, drinking iced tea and chatting about inconsequential things like the traffic on the nearby highway or the more weighty matters of living peacefully in a family of eleven children. It was a good time. A good way to ease from day to night.

In our mobile, electrically lighted society, many of us could use a small portion of this sanity of the evening. Absorbed with keeping up with the Millers and Yoders, the Goldmans and Schumanns, the Bensons and Browns, we are more likely to spend our evenings in fast-forward replay, racing from dinner on the run to shopping at the mall. Soccer practice to baby showers. Prayer meetings to power restaurants. Maybe we make it home by ten or eleven. Maybe we don't.

It's different for my people. Keeping up with the Stoltzfuses and Beilers does not include eating out three times a week. It doesn't include making sure the children get to Little League or piano lessons. It doesn't include evening church activities and prayer meetings. There are pressures, to be sure, but most Amish women are not willing to sacrifice their love of quiet evenings for the hectic schedules of the fast-forward life.

While they understand that the forces guiding our lives are very different, they hope we, too, will make time to walk in the snow or watch the sun go down. They hope we will talk ourselves and our children into easing out of the mad schedules driven by the expectations of other people—our employers and friends, our co-workers, schoolmates, and cousins. They hope we will feel the joy, the calm, easy rest of evening.

The Blessings of Simple Communication— Snail Mail and E-Mail

> 'Why is it that you can sometimes feel the reality of people more keenly through a letter than face to face?
> —ANNE MORROW LINDBERGH,
> *Bring Me a Unicorn (1972)*

If there is one thing we can learn from the growing appreciation many of us have for sending messages by electronic mail, it is that my people were right. The telephone is a poor substitute for written communication. It is less satisfying, more invasive, and much noisier. This is what Amish women have been saying for several generations. Although they often long for (and sometimes bend the rules to have) easy access to telephones, they also have great sympathy for the church's position that telephones should be kept outside the home because they disrupt the quiet meter of daily life, the rhythms of work and conversation. Communicating by telephone, my people have said, cannot compete with words written on a page, with the satisfaction of rereading a sentence or paragraph to discover a shade of meaning not seen or felt before.

The world, so captured by the romance of instant communication, has taken much longer to register these truths. We are still, and probably always will be, enthralled by the telephone and its immediacy. Phones in the kitchen. Phones in the bedroom. Phones at the office. Phones by the cashier's counter. Hand-held phones. Car phones. Cell phones. We love them all. And carry them with us in our purses and jacket pockets. (Is there anything more annoying than a private cell phone ringing *and being answered* in the middle of a bookstore, grocery line, library, or restaurant?)

My people have kept their lives from becoming so cluttered by limiting access. In most Amish communities, the general guideline goes like this, "Keep them outside the home, in a barn or small shed.

Use an answering machine. Do not let telephones take over your life." Those of us overcome by the encompassing presence of telephones long for the same lack of clutter, the same simple choices.

Which brings us to the connection between snail mail and e-mail. My people have always considered the written word a vital form of communication—letters, notes, greeting cards, and postcards. Many of us agree. These simple touches let others know we think of them without interrupting or upending their schedules. Often, though, we choose telephones for their convenience and quickness.

What we need is a more convenient way to write letters. That is the blessing of electronic mail. It takes essentially the same time and energy to compose an e-mail version of snail mail, but thanks to the personal computer and the Internet, e-mail can be delivered much more quickly.

Is it not a wonderful twist of fate that the very piece of equipment once thought to signal the end of words on a page has become a possible means for their preservation? The telephone and instant communication have been among the defining elements of the twentieth-century experience. Perhaps in the twenty-first century, we will concern ourselves more with preserving words and the discipline of thought as the Internet and online services make written communication as easy as dialing a telephone number. An amazing possibility and evidence, I think, of the resilience of the human spirit. As soon as we predict the demise of something as essential to human experience as the written word, some ingenious mind develops a way to revive its use.

I expect Amish women will stick to snail mail and limited telephone access. Most are as unimpressed by the personal computer, online services, and electronic mail as they were by the telephone. In the meantime, we might take a small step toward simplifying our lives by agreeing with them about the telephone while composing more snail mail and, if we have the technology, e-mail letters and messages.

The Amish Were Right about Progress

Whoever said progress was a positive thing has never been to Florida or California.

—RITA MAE BROWN,
Bingo (1988)

Change is inevitable. Change can be either positive or negative. Change does not equal progress. A thesaurus, dictionary, pens, and paper work as well for a writer as a word-processing system on a personal computer. The computer does not improve writing; it changes how one writes, but it does not inherently improve writing. A horse and buggy work as well for transportation as a car. The car does not improve driving; it changes how one drives, but it does not inherently improve driving. These are the fundamental principles about technology, invention, and change that my people teach in their homes, churches, and schools. They accept change, but they are suspicious of its supposed connections to progress.

Indeed, the American love affair with progress was one of the reasons my people were so opposed to the consolidation of schools. They had no reason to believe their children would receive better educations in large, central systems than they had been getting all along in neighborhood country schools. My people were right. The themes and ideas advanced by the educational revolution of the 1940s and 1950s were not better. They were only different. And they also happened to be diametrically at odds with the Amish way.

I went to a one-room Amish school for the first five years. We moved, and my parents, who felt the Amish school was too far away, decided to send us to public schools, where I stayed through tenth grade. I remember hearing about the continuing evolution of humankind, with its promise that people would be much kinder and better to each other somewhere in the future, possibly by the year 2000. I remember hearing that technology would so improve our lives that we could look forward to a future of relative ease and relaxation. I remember wondering about these notions and occasionally asking my parents what they thought. They assured me there was no evidence to support the idea that evolution and progress would make us better people or the world a better place.

Is it not telling that, instead of realizing growing improvements, the world has suffered through an unparalleled escalation of blue- and white-collar crime, increasing environmental challenges, and ever more legitimate questions about the influences of technology and modernization?

Even so, many of us have such faith in progress that we never raise an eyebrow when someone falls back on the tried-and-true phrase that signals that a particular idea, behavior, or belief system is behind the times: "It's 1998, after all!" This exclamation (which of course changes with the year) always implies there are no rational reasons for not embracing modernity and change, no rational reasons for driving horses or writing letters with pen and paper. The argument goes, "We have the technology. We have the knowledge. Therefore, we have no excuse for not using it to improve our lives."

LOUISE STOLTZFUS

❧ ❧

Women among my people beg to differ. In their eyes, there are many reasons for not driving cars or using computers. They interfere with plain and simple living. They do not make life easier or better. They change our circumstances, sometimes in positive ways and sometimes in negative ways, but they do not improve the quality of life.

Perhaps we women of the world might also consider the Amish way. We might place less confidence in the devices and inventions of the human mind. We might become less certain that progress provides a remedy for life's ills.

Laughter,
the Elixir of Life

There is a time for everything,
A time to weep and a time to laugh,
A time to mourn and a time to dance.
—*Book of Ecclesiastes*

Whenever I hit a dry season, I realize how important laughter is to wellness. A healing balm, better than any medication, it changes the chemical composition of the brain, releases stress, and binds us to our children and companions. A good laugh lightens the moment, opens the door to better communication, and keeps the everyday grind of work and home from consuming our spirits.

I grew up with people who loved to laugh. My mother. My mother's people. My father's parents. These people had hardships, many of them, but they always believed in "a time to laugh." They were great fun. Holidays were often filled with mirth. Family get-togethers were laced with the joy of each other's company.

Given the history of my mother's people, my memories of the many good times are especially poignant. These women and men could only laugh because they made conscious choices to overcome the tragic effects of shattering imperfections and a father whose mental illness interfered with opportunities for happiness. They talked about it, wept together when they needed to, but then also laughed together. Today, my nieces and nephews look on with surprise and delight when my mother, their aging grandmother, dissolves into gales of laughter. It doesn't happen often enough. For any of us.

The rigid straightness projected by Amish women in public seldom holds up in their homes or among friends. Children giggle with delight. Young people smile and laugh at each other's jokes. Middle-aged women tell amusing stories while quilting, baking cookies, or preparing meals.

A life without laughter, most Amish women believe, is no life at all. Lydia puts it succinctly for me. "We laugh at ourselves and at each other. Doesn't the Bible say, 'a time to weep and a time to laugh'?"

Laughing at ourselves is never easy. Much of humor has its basis in the potential pain it brings to someone else. We laugh at practical jokes like moving a co-worker's car precisely because the person will panic. "Oh no, what happened to my car? Was it stolen? What am I going to do!" We find such panic funny. We laugh at ethnic jokes (although most of us know better) because they put whole cultures into an embarrassing light. We laugh freely at other people.

But our own foibles are sometimes harder to take lightly. Think about the most embarrassing thing that happened to you in the past year. Ask yourself whether you can laugh about it. Try. It's a learned behavior and may well be the elixir of life.

Indeed, laughter has been known to prolong life. To work as well as Prozac for relieving the pains of depression. To move us from an obsession with the absence of perfection to higher levels of personal acceptance. To make us easier to live with and much more fun to be around. It's just that simple. Laugh.

Women
and the Scent
of a Farm

They are much to be pitied who have not been given a taste for nature in early life.
—JANE AUSTEN,
Mansfield Park (1814)

arms do not necessarily smell good. Especially not to the untrained olfactory nerve. To the trained nerve, though, there is a certain pleasantness about the smell of cows, chickens, or even hogs. Each has its own essence. And women who live on farms, whether Amish or not, learn to appreciate each scent for its own qualities. We cannot forget. We carry with us the memories of each one.

There is the strong, fuzzy closeness of the cow. When you milk a cow by hand, you nestle your head in the hollow just in front of her right rear leg. You feel her tactile, velvety skin, and the smell goes with you forever.

There is the sharp edginess of the chicken. When you enter a free-range chicken house, you dump the feed first to distract the hens. Then you retrieve the eggs, still jerking hands and feet free of the pecking, busy beaks. You seldom cuddle chickens, but you always remember their peculiar odor.

There is the overwhelming, air-filling scent of the hog. This animal wallows in mud, appearing to have little regard for common standards of cleanliness. Still, many hog farmers, their wives and children, like coming home to the smell of their hogs.

It's all a matter of perception, I guess. Many farmers find the scent of the city deeply offensive. Smog, tightly closed buildings, and piles of garbage make these women and men long for the wide-open spaces and fresh air of their country homes, for the comforting smell of cows, chickens, and hogs. This is true for Amish women.

Amused by the shock and displeasure of those whose romantic notions of Amish life do not include the scent of a farm, my people are inclined to smile as much at us as we may smile at them for not enjoying the scent of the city. Or for not appreciating the expected *absence* of scent in suburbia.

Which is where the battle lines of scent are often drawn. Those who purchase tract houses backed by open fields and Amish farms with the expectation never to smell cows, chickens, or hogs are usually in for a rude awakening. Farmers spread manure. They have to. They fertilize their land to grow crops. Their crops and produce fill our grocery stores. Without their fertilizer, our suburban paradises would ultimately have no food.

Farms may be smelly, but they are also filled with delightful aromas, scents enjoyed by women of the farm, women of the city, and women of the suburbs. Consider the biting sweetness of new-mown hay, the earthiness of freshly plowed fields, the ripening broadness of home-grown tomatoes, and the lightness of lilies of the valley or wild-honeysuckle vines perfuming the early evening air. Together we breathe deeply and give thanks for clean air and open spaces. We give thanks for the scent of a farm.

The Old Farmers' Almanac and My Grandmother's Garden

Gardening is an exercise in optimism. Sometimes, it is the triumph of hope over experience.
—MARINA SCHINZ,
Visions of Paradise (1985)

Gardening serves more than one purpose for Amish women. It's a source of pleasure. A source of food. And a source of income. In the early spring, women among my people compete with each other to see who will be the first to plant peas, gather lettuce, or put out tomatoes. They have a great time talking about the best place to buy seeds, how the soil should feel before planting, and what the *Farmers' Almanac* says about successful gardening.

My paternal grandmother loved the almanac. She planted peas and tomatoes according to the stages of the moon, reminding her children to do the same. She paid attention to frost tables, growing seasons, and weather forecasts. On many an early spring day, we would all perk up as she pulled this fascinating gardener's bible from her magazine rack and began reading its predictions and laughing over its adages and proverbs.

I haven't read an almanac since she died, which might help explain my less productive forays into gardening. She gardened to fill her kitchen, pantry, and cellar with another year's supply of food. In the tiny (by her standards), square-yard plots of the small green space behind my rowhouse, I garden primarily for pleasure. I've had cucumbers go wild on the fence, tomatoes yield with a vengeance, eggplant succumb to bugs. If my grandmother were here, she'd probably murmur with pleasure over the tomatoes and advise me to pick the bugs off the eggplant before they take over.

She was like most other Amish women for whom gardening is also work. Fresh food for the table cannot be realized without the back-breaking toil of hoeing weeds or keeping pests at bay. Without getting up early in the morning to care for the ground and plants in those hours before the sun turns hot. Without worrying about dry weather or strawberries that rot on the vine because of too much rain.

An Amish woman's garden is her kingdom. A measure of her worth to the family. She may not earn a salary, but she saves thousands of dollars a year because she plants and picks bushels of peas and green beans, dozens of ears of corn, and prodigious quantities of red beets, cabbage, onions, lettuce, peppers, cauliflower, and cantaloupe. All of which she either serves fresh, freezes, or cans, lining her cellar shelves with a stunning array of colorful brined and pickled fare.

Annie loves few things more than walking through her garden in the mid-morning hours, filling her apron with the fruits of whatever plants happen to be bearing. "I think I can feed my family better from my garden than I ever could if we bought everything at the grocery store." She and her husband make a point of buying groceries no more than once every other month, when they stock up on bulk supplies of staples such as noodles, cereal, and flour. In the wintertime, Annie's mid-morning trek takes her to the basement and her stock of canned goods as she plans her family's large noon meal.

The garden as a source of income? I never imagined it would work for me until I lost my job at the height of summer several years ago. Suddenly, the cost of groceries mattered. I discovered that my miniature backyard garden with its abundant supply (that year) of tomatoes, zucchini, and cucumbers dressed up many a meal. I even managed to rescue one eggplant from the bugs, savoring a supper of fried slices, first dipped in egg and cracker crumbs, just the way my grandmother always fixed this unique and delicious vegetable. I'm sure she would have been happy for me.

An Amish
Prayer Life

*P*rayer is the language of the heart.
—GRACE AGUILAR,
The Spirit of Judaism (1842)

Prayer. It is a private communication between a woman and her God. Or a man and his God. It does not require flowery language. It is not for public consumption or display. My people rarely intercede with God in full view of each other or the world, a custom that sometimes unnerves those who expect the Amish to have a broader acceptance of the traditional patterns of public prayer. Most Amish women and men prefer their private prayers to the extemporaneous offerings so common in many other Christian traditions.

We women of the world may find ourselves in tune with the Amish way. We scarcely have room in our lives for conversation with each other, much less, audible conversation with God. We don't have time to stop for fifteen minutes every morning or evening to intercede aloud before God. Perhaps we have given up on prayer because it seems an archaic or artificial way of talking about our problems.

Amish women have not given up on prayer, but they rarely feel the need to give impromptu spoken prayers before meals, in a moment of crisis, or as a scheduled part of religious gatherings. They are more inclined toward something they call "having a prayerful attitude." This kind of prayer can happen in a garden among lilies and roses. It can happen at a sewing machine with colorful pieces of fabric. It can happen in a kitchen among pots and pans as the peculiar fragrance of a lovely roast fills the air.

We do not always need a physical posture of prayer. We only need a prayerful attitude, a thoughtful space, and the silence or noise of the world around us. We can pray on a train. In a traffic jam. While listening to music. While watching a movie. While holding a friend. Everywhere, anytime, we can connect to the calming and transforming energy of a prayerful life. Such is the beauty and wonder of learning to pray in the moment.

Beyond their reliance on having a prayerful attitude, women among my people also connect with the liturgical cadence of written German prayers. These prayers and the books from which they are taken are as important a religious treasure to my people as their Bibles and hymn books. Many Amish families end their day with the father reading an evening prayer. Often recited in the breathless, singsong style of a poet reading her own words, these written German prayers take root in the soul and spirit of many an Amish child and young person. We who were once Amish often find ourselves remembering.

When I was seven years old, my grandfather gave me a German children's prayer book. I had forgotten it until I renovated a room about a year ago. There on an old bookshelf, I found the long-lost gem. Opening the pages, I was transported to my grandparents' home and the words of their late-evening prayers. Once again, I heard the inflections in my grandfather's voice rising and falling as we knelt nearby: *"Ach, bleib beh uns, Herr Jesu Christ, weil es nun Abend worden ist"* (Oh, stay with us Lord Jesus Christ, throughout the evening which has come). How lucky for me that he chose to read his prayers. How glad I am to have this clear memory of him speaking these words.

The Nudgings of God

*T*he soul is kissed by God in its innermost regions.
　　　　　—HILDEGARD OF BINGEN,
　　　　　Scivias (1150)

*I*t's a commonly voiced litany: "I'm just so busy." And it's become a sort of catch phrase in the iconography of our time. I find myself repeating it to some sympathetic soul at least two or three times a week, often in a beleagured tone, my eyes rolling and my body sighing.

Ours is a world with precious little space for contemplative thought and connecting to the mysterious workings of God. We don't have time for silence. Time for ourselves. Or time for each other. Often, it takes a crisis, in its unwelcome way, to stop our forward motion. In those moments we retreat and reach out, sometimes calling on a God outside ourselves. A God for the extraordinary.

What then about a God within, God for the ordinary? When I ask my people about their concept of God, they are inclined to respond, as Rachel does, with a story. Her story is a collection of crazy-quilt patches beginning some years ago while she worked at a farm supply center as a secretary. "One of my friends came to me one day asking whether I had heard about the new clinic and the doctor who would run it. It would be a place where families could take children with genetics-related disorders and get treatment at affordable rates."

Her story expands, slowly taking on its distinctive shape. "My friend asked, 'Why don't you work there?' First, I just said no. It's not for me. But that's when God started nudging me.

"Three different things happened. First, a Mennonite woman who had come into our office asked if I had heard about the clinic. Several days later, I ran into an acquaintance on the street. Again, the question came out of the blue, 'Have you heard about the clinic?' I asked myself, 'God, does this mean something? What do you want me to do?' "

As I listen, Rachel pulls out the final patch of her story and binds it to her decision and the joy-filled freedom of following this ordinary God. "My job included calling people with overdue balances. One morning as I worked through my list, I talked for a while with a man I knew and trusted. He explained that they could not pay their bill because of a sick child and the medical bills that had upset their family finances. Then he, too, asked whether I had heard about the new clinic. That man and his story assured me that God was speaking. I changed my mind and went to work at the clinic. I've never been sorry." Rachel believes God is concerned with the ordinary events of the everyday.

For me her story also raises questions: "Who is God? What is God like?" Questions that occur to all of us. Questions we may sometimes choose not to entertain. Questions, nevertheless, whose answers determine and guide the course of our lives. What could be more tender and wise than a God who speaks to us in conversation and interaction with other people? A God who meets us in the eyes and hands of a friend. A God whose love we feel when we are held and cared for by a parent. A God who gives us gentle nudges in new directions. A God who calms the body and kisses the soul, infusing us with the quiet confidence and strength we need to sustain our busy lives.

Yield Not to Temptation

Watch and pray so that you will not fall into temptation. The spirit is willing, but the body is weak.

—JESUS,
Book of Matthew

You cannot avoid temptation, but you can decide not to
yield. This teaching pervades Amish culture. Few women
or men are able to avoid it long enough to turn the perfectly
useful energies of money, power, and sex into vices. Those
who give in to the seduction of too much are definitely not admired

in the same way the rest of us might admire the Vanderbilts, Trumps, Marilyn Monroes, or Madonnas. Rather, Amish parents admonish their children not to be like them.

From the first moment with candy bars in a store to the day we feel like stealing from an employer because, after all, we're not paid enough, the battles of the conscience rage on. We never move beyond the need for self-awareness. How we respond to our consciences most likely depends on what our parents and mentors taught us about the allure of temptation.

About money, my parents were very clear. Do not steal. Always pay your bills on time. And learn to know when enough is enough. This is how they lived. Sometimes with a measure of anxiety and what certainly felt like *less* than enough. But always with integrity and a holistic view of how to make and spend money. You desired enough to clothe, feed, and house yourself and your family. You spent it for necessities, saved a few dollars, and gave the rest away.

On the subject of power, they were also vocal and certain. Do not yield to the desire for individual glory. Too much reverence or power directed to one person undermines the nature of the gathered community. Long before I heard the phrase "Absolute power corrupts absolutely," my parents championed its principles by example and practice.

About sex? Well, about sex they whispered. By their lives they showed us it was for those committed to each other in marriage. For love. Never for selling a product or wielding authority over another person. Never to inflict pain. But always to realize mutual pleasure and love between two people.

They were not perfect. And the times they yielded to temptation became object lessons that we, their eleven children, have carried with us through life. We find ourselves repeating their words of wisdom to each other and our children. As my father said hundreds of times, "Temptation will come. What you do with the temptation—that will determine the course of your life."

When we, the women of the world, catch ourselves on the verge of yielding to temptation, we might rather stop to reassess our priorities. Not yielding may affect pocketbooks. Places on the corporate ladder. And momentary gratification. But it will never keep us from happiness. It will never rob us of peace. The result of not yielding to temptation—peace and happiness—advances wholeness and makes the world a better place.

LOUISE STOLTZFUS

❧ ❧

121

Faith in Action

$\mathcal{W}$e have too many high sounding words, and too few actions that correspond with them.

—ABIGAIL ADAMS,
letter (1774)

hat we do reveals so much more about who we are than what we say. This is the standard by which Amish women measure faithfulness. Spirituality cannot be defined by words alone; it must also be supported by actions and behaviors. We must do more than say "I love you." More than make promises. More than speak platitudes.

All the "I love you"s in the world cannot heal a broken relationship. Only the slow dance of living peacefully with another person, the everyday kindnesses of washing dishes and cleaning bathrooms, communicates the gentle touch necessary to restore a lost connection between two people.

All the promises in the world do not make it possible to live with integrity. Only the painstaking work of keeping promises or taking responsibility for not keeping promises defines what we really think about personal accountability.

All the religious platitudes in the world do not make faith appealing. Only the actions of a faithful life—respect, reverence, understanding—attract others to discipleship and service. Many Amish women believe how they live is much more important than witnessing or sharing their faith with others.

This peculiar penchant for actions rather than words has led many well-meaning Christians to conclude that my people are not truly Christian. After all, it is often noted, Jesus requested us to "go into all the world." Sometimes, my people are influenced by these persistent words about evangelism. (They leave the Amish and join more evangelical groups.)

More often they view these words and thought processes through a different-colored lens. They believe Jesus meant for them to live above reproach in the eyes of the world. This is what they hope to do. To live above reproach, as much as humanly possible, in full view of their own community and the rest of society.

I think my people offer a refreshing perspective to a world constantly torn by religious differences and tension. Their ability to live faithfully without feeling the need to convert others may actually be a light that shines as brightly and blesses as many souls as the elaborate mission programs and outreaches of many other denominations.

While most Christian groups conduct their missions with thoughtfulness and care, the efforts to convince others of the absolute rightness of a particular way of life through rhetoric rather than respectful living nearly always results in tragedy. Long-standing disputes fueled by religious discord give all of us reason to wonder about the wisdom of witnessing, the wisdom of pushing our own religious agenda.

Take the age-old dispute between Catholics and Protestants in Northern Ireland. The ethnic wars between Muslims and Christians in eastern Europe. The ongoing hate crimes against Jews throughout the world. And the attacks on black churches in America.

These stories make reconsidering the rhetoric that divides one religious group from another an essential exercise of civilization. How much better to touch others through faithful living, respectful overtures, and careful restoration. How much more healing and hopeful these quiet revelations of spirituality and living well. For as my maternal grandmother often reminded us, "Actions speak louder than words."

The Lord Helps Those
Who Help Themselves

How can a rational being be ennobled by anything
that is not obtained by its *own* exertions?
—MARY WOLLSTONECRAFT,
A Vindication of the Rights of Woman (1792)

In a culture that prizes freedom and independence as much as
the American culture, it's both fascinating and remarkable to
find so many women bound up in the addictions of co-
dependent relationships. Why is this? we wonder. How do

we become so involved in pleasing others? How can we regain a balance that frees us to take care of ourselves?

My maternal grandmother, a tender woman with a proverb for most every situation, used to say, "The Lord helps those who help themselves." On the surface, her story scarcely supports the proverb. She married at twenty-four and gave birth to fourteen children in twenty-one years. She lost a seven-month-old daughter to a heart defect. She could not understand her husband and his wild swings between gentle, caring paternal feeling and a temper he refused to control. She grieved his loss for years before he finally died of cancer in the twenty-seventh year of their marriage. Through it all, she tried to help herself, supporting the family with various sewing projects and relying on the goodwill of her gathered community.

By the time I knew her, she was an old woman. She was also a survivor. A woman who had picked up the pieces of her life and moved on. A woman who had survived because she exercised a self-sufficiency that allowed her to turn to her community. Had she turned to an opposite impulse—absolute freedom—she would have refused the gifts of money and emotional support from her community and tied herself so completely to the failure and loss of her husband's tragic life that she could not have gone on. When she said, "The Lord helps those who help themselves," she was acknowledging the thin line between giving up and going on.

Women like my grandmother leave an important legacy. The legacy of going to our communities for help. Of telling our stories. Of willingly admitting we cannot solve our problems alone. Almost without exception, we will be blessed by friends and family members who come forward with shoulders to cry on, money to tide us over, and advice for how to get back on our feet.

These women also pass on a legacy of self-sufficiency. Of going within to find the resources to recover from loss. Of believing in ourselves and our own strength. Of working hard and living independently. The harmony we find in balancing self-sufficiency with the ability to receive from others fills our lives with hope and the assurance that the Lord, indeed, helps those who help themselves.

My grandmother's story also sheds light on how a culture defined by freedom manages to bind so many of us in the grips of co-dependent relationships. In the far reaches of freedom, we proclaim ourselves independent of others, not needing family, friends, or a support system. Because this expression of freedom disconnects us from vital gifts and friendships, we often turn instead to less than helpful, co-dependent relationships. With a husband sometimes. A mother or a sister. Or a whole series of responsibilities to people who give us nothing in return.

May we rise up. Find the strength, as my grandmother did, to call on family and friends when emotional and physical needs overwhelm us. But also find the courage to take care of ourselves, to believe ourselves sufficient and strong. Women with hope. Women with dignity. Women with true freedom.

The Hope of Salvation

*F*or we are saved by hope.
—*Book of the Ephesians*

*L*ike most people who subscribe to contemplative expressions of faith, my people believe that salvation and redemption depend on an external power as well as a strong inner life. To them faith is about the simple wisdom born of surrender. It is about love and hope, simplicity and serenity. Complex theological interpretations of biblical teachings do not interest most Amish women or men.

Lydia tells me, "My parents did not hit us over the head with the Bible. They read the Bible and often talked about the love of God. They told us that being a Christian was a very personal thing. Everything you do, they said, reflects what you believe."

Ada says, "We Amish have what we call the hope of salvation."

Women like Ada and Lydia identify with an old, but also fascinating, translation of redemption. Redemption is not a once and done experience; it is a process. It involves a lifetime of kind and thoughtful living. A lifetime of renewal and regeneration. A lifetime of self-awareness and receiving from others.

Redemption is not about deciphering arcane and difficult words of scripture. It is about treating others with consideration and respect. It is about waking up each day with a desire to improve ourselves. It is about going to sleep at night with a simple, peaceful heart, knowing we have made mistakes but confident we can do better tomorrow. I find the Amish view of salvation and redemption to be both extraordinarily plain and completely original.

What I find original about the Amish way reflects my personal truth, a truth born in the teachings and spiritual language of my people. Like them, I also do not think redemption begins and ends with an emotional trek to the altar. I believe salvation involves a lifetime of sincerity and doing unto others as we would have others do unto us. This is what my people mean by the hope of salvation.

It's an uncomplicated, easy way to think about faith. Sustenance for the soul resides in the hope of salvation. In the willingness to say, "Today I did not treat others well," but also to say, "Today I will forgive myself because I have the hope of salvation, the strength to do better tomorrow." Whatever our understanding of faith, may we all find ways to engage ourselves in the hope and process of redemption.

An Amish Guide to Fashion

*T*heir dress is very independent of fashion.
—ELIZABETH GASKELL,
Cranford (1851)

There are three elements of fashion—neatness, comfort, and simplicity—that I learned from my people and wanted to bring with me into the world. Sometimes I have succeeded. Sometimes not.

I have always been a bit more carefree and offhand about my appearance than my mother would have liked. I refused to wear a perfectly lovely pink dress she made when I was four or five years old. I hated to sew and dissolved in tears over many a dress, apron, or jacket project through the years. I never could be content, my mother says, with Amish styles and patterns. I have not, however, forgotten or abandoned the essential wisdom about clothing and looking good that she imparted to me.

Amish women like my mother often exclaim over the lack of common sense that, in their view, sustains high fashion. The money is beyond their comprehension. The patterns are not neat, comfortable, or simple. *Why?* they wonder among themselves. Why would any woman subject herself to the indignities many popular fashions create? The tugging required to keep a short skirt from venturing into immodesty seems pointless to them. As do high heels, dangling earrings, and bare-shouldered gowns with vast, swirling skirts.

This does not mean they are not style conscious. Every culture has its own fashion expectations and requirements, and my people are no exception. They care about how they look. They do not all wear black. They have individual color and style preferences. They enjoy shopping. And they talk about styles and fashions among themselves.

"Did you see that new dress Sadie had on? Wasn't that a nice shade of purple?"

"How did you sew those sleeves?" or "How do you get the hem to stay so even?"

"I'd like to have some of that new fabric. Where did you get it? It looks really comfortable for summer."

My people desire and wear fashionable clothing, but they interpret style and fashion through a different set of cultural parameters. They have no L.L. Bean or Oscar de la Renta. No Donna Karan or Calvin Klein. No brand names and no ready-to-wear clothing. To these women, high and proper fashion means busy sewing machines, solid-colored, store-bought fabrics, and patterns passed down from generation to generation.

They utterly do not understand fashion shows and would never consider modeling, but their trained eyes often spot changes in the dresses, aprons, and capes of their own people. Those with an eye for the fancy pick up the changes in future sewing projects, often starting a mini–fashion trend in the community. Those with an eye for the plain admonish each other not to yield to such temptation.

Most—whether plain or fancy in their dress—are convinced the requirements of their community bring them distinct fashion advantages over many other women. These rules and expectations, my people believe, give them the freedom to hold tenaciously to common standards of simplicity, comfort, and neatness. They wish the same for us, the women of the world.

And why not? Perhaps if we began refusing to purchase shoes that hurt our feet, the designers would no longer produce them. If we ignored complicated and uncomfortable new fashions, the Karans and Kleins might get the message. If we determined to buy clothing only on the premise of comfort, we might be surprised to find it also makes us look good. Really good.

Changing our focus from "what's in this season" to comfort and neatness might actually lead to greater simplicity. It would definitely lower stress levels, because we'd give much less of our precious time and energy trying to look better than other women. We'd have easier lives. That's what Amish women like my mother believe.

Banjoes, Fiddles, and Barns

*I*n no order of things is adolescence a time of the simple life.

—JANET ERSKINE STUART,
letter (1922)

*M*y people have a rather unusual and very healthy, it seems to me, point of view about self-expression among the young. They believe young people should have opportunities, as they say, "to sow their wild oats."

It's a rite of passage Amish children await with great eagerness. Its secrets are whispered in one-room schools, where excited little girls tell stories of an older sister's boyfriend and posturing little boys brag about the brand-new horse and buggy they will receive when they reach the magic age. Sixteen.

The subject generates lots of heated debate in the kitchens, shops, and milking houses of Amish families. I have heard many women say, with great concern, that allowing young people to choose new friends and make some of their own decisions is one thing. Too much freedom, on the other hand, is very different. Some fear that over-emphasizing the "sowing wild oats" philosophy creates far too many problems for the young.

As is true in many subcultures, the Amish have their secrets. There is none they guard more zealously than the questions "How do the young people sow wild oats? What do you mean?" Most prefer not to explain. Instead, they speak of teaching their children the differences between right and wrong. "If we teach them well," they say, "the young people will not forsake the truth."

Parents who succeed in building a firm foundation can afford to extend freedom, opening the doors to responsible experimentation with the newfound pleasures of emerging adulthood. "If you let them sow their wild oats when they are young, they will come back and be stronger Amish people. We think the young people should be allowed to have their fun. But we also think they should realize that fun can be carried too far." Sadie's comments are echoed in the refrain of many, many Amish women when they talk about the responsibilities and trials of raising teenagers. What they repeatedly say to each other is, "We must warn them of the dangers of going too far, of not being responsible and careful. We must teach them that their actions do have consequences."

I am often impressed by how close these words of wisdom come to textbook advice on guiding teenagers of any culture into whole and happy lives. We pray. We plead occasionally. We do our best to guide them gently, and we rejoice when they come to us in both the bad and good times.

What secrets, then, about their young people are Amish women protecting from the public eye? I'm not sure I know. Which is, of course, the point. I think it's probably the three-prong, universal stuff of youth culture—experimenting with drugs, music, and sex.

I think many parents manage to shelter their young people from most of these activities. My parents did. I suspect those who don't feel the confusion and embarrassment most parents feel when "wild oats" go out of control. Most of the time, though, an Amish young person's wild times are manageable and even creative.

Hoedowns happen. Complete with banjoes and fiddles and drums, these vigorous barn dances shake the floor and rattle the rafters. Scores of young men and women, most dressed in traditional Amish garb, promenade, form a square, and swing their partners with a grace and style not unlike Nashville's own and the best of the Grand Ole Opry.

These kids know how to have a good time. They date. They play volleyball and baseball and ice hockey. They have skating parties and taffy pulls and hymn singings. They flirt and fall in love. They break up and hate each other. They hang out with friends. They are troubled by life, as teenagers everywhere are, and when they come home to their parents, they seek solid ground.

Like mothers everywhere, women among my people give many hours of gentle and firm counsel, spend long nights in sleepless worry, and rejoice for years when the children "turn out right."

The Mores of Courting and Being Together

I've figured out why first dates don't work any better than they do. It's because they take place in restaurants. Women are weird and confused and unhappy about food, and men are weird and confused and unhappy about money, yet off they go, the minute they meet, to where you use money to buy food.

—ADAIR LARA,
Welcome to Earth, Mom (1992)

*I*n the days of Louisa May Alcott, Jane Austen, and the Brontë sisters, people called it courting. Today, in the time of Barbara Kingsolver, Jane Smiley, and Anne Tyler, we call it going out. "Who are you going out with these days?"

We've invented a language for talking about the intricacies of love and getting together. "Are you seeing anyone?" "Can I take you out to lunch? Or dinner? Or a movie?" "I want us to be friends." "I need a commitment." "I want a relationship." "I want to be with you." The only thing that hasn't changed is "Will you marry me?" Unless, of course, we consider Hugh Grant's memorable nonproposal in the last frame of *Four Weddings and a Funeral*. "I was wondering if you could agree never to marry me. And if you think you might want to do that for the rest of your life."

It's a language my people cannot comprehend. And it's not just because they don't go to the movies or read Kingsolver, Smiley, and Tyler. They hold very different notions about courting and relationships. Some I agree with. Some I wonder about. Some, I admit, I find completely mystifying.

The idea that young teenagers should not date has always made a lot of sense to me. Somewhere in their history, my people settled on age sixteen, a tradition they've followed for many generations. Few of us will argue with the point that the struggles of those going through puberty seldom prepare them to work on the problems of young love.

Amish young people have their dates at home in the family living room or kitchen. They rarely go out because most parents consider restaurants too expensive and too public. A mother of six, Ada reflects on the restaurant question: "We want our young people to date at home, where we can see what they're doing. Why go out in public? Why spend money for a restaurant when you can have better food at home?" She smiles. As do I. I understand her position, but if I had teenagers, I'm sure I would prefer they found a middle ground—time together at home but also time away from home.

Young Amish men and women, though they sometimes resist, are taught never to date anyone outside their faith. This practice mirrors an argument many parents make to their children. For me it always raises concerns about narrow-mindedness and closed doors.

When Amish young people date those who are not Amish, some parents are willing to accept the choice. Others cajole, cry, and plead for their children to "find an Amish boy or girl." To my people, it's a question of community. You can marry an outsider if he or she agrees to become Amish—a conversion argument parents of many faiths make to their children. I have never understood it.

Whatever the mores that guide our own culture and its courting practices, may we have the simple wisdom to accept each other and the decisions our children make. Even when they are very different from our own.

In Praise
of Weddings

O Gott Vater, wir loben dich
und deine Güte preisen,
die du, O Herr, so gnadiglich
an uns neu hast bewiesen;
und hast uns, Herr, zusammen geführt
uns zu ermahnen durch dein Wort.
Gib uns Genad zu diesem!*
—*Ausbund*

* See page 360 for an English translation.

Most Amish weddings open with a Gregorian chant-like recitation of this ancient German hymn, "*O Gott Vater*," also called *Das Lob Lied*, or the praise song. "*Das Lob Lied*," which is sung as the bride and groom move into the room, embodies the message and mystique of so much about my people and sets the tone for all that transpires as the wedding liturgy moves from its morning service of worship into an afternoon of praise and a long evening of merrymaking.

An aura of radiant energy surrounds many Amish wedding ceremonies. It's a radiance nurtured in the cadence of tradition where everyone knows what to expect and what to do. Like Tevye in *Fiddler on the Roof*, Amish fathers want their daughters and sons to marry in the ways and customs of the foremothers and fathers. Tradition, tradition, tradition. It's a word as often heard in most Amish households as it is in the great musical. It's also a concept all of us may want to consider for its possibilities and for the vision it adds to any ceremony, whether Jewish, African, Baptist, Italian, Catholic, Irish, or Amish. For radiance grows from embracing our heritage and so recognizing its intrinsic gifts and grace.

None of the glitz and glamour of stress-inducing contemporary weddings can be found in an Amish couple's plans for marriage. Imagine not having to find and pay for a church, reception hall, cake, flowers, candles, or photographers. Amish young people have their weddings at home. The bride's parents pay for the food, and special friends bring cakes, candies, and other decorated desserts as gifts. Imagine not having to spend hours choosing gowns and tuxedos. Amish couples wear new clothing, sewn according to their comfortable, Sunday dress patterns. Their wedding clothes are practical and traditional.

Imagine also the sense of wonder when such reverence for tradition yields itself to soothing spiritual moments and lots of fun. That is what happens at many Amish weddings. Few of the rituals of plain life lend themselves to larger celebration and more pure joy. Surrounded by the mystery and fire of young love, these gatherings bring together the equal and opposite impulses of so much about my people.

The Amish way demands a certain austerity. And it is this manner of living that dictates every wedding begin very early in the morning (8:00 A.M. usually) and proceed with a four-hour prescribed service, punctuated with the slow intonation of hymns, two long sermons, scripture readings, and wedding prayers. The guests sit quietly on hard, backless benches, arranged throughout the first-floor rooms of the bride's family home, often a large farmhouse.

LOUISE STOLTZFUS

❀ ❀

The Amish way also allows, and even invites, a certain gaiety and lightness of being. It is this manner of living that takes over in the minutes and hours after the two young people receive the marriage pronouncement and blessing. The solemn ceremony comes to an end. Suddenly, the farmhouse is alive with conversation and camaraderie. Faces light up. Jokes abound. The air becomes charged and full of life and fun. To the great puzzlement of an occasional guest who is not Amish, the hard benches are transformed into long tables, set up on wooden trestles and covered with white cloth, exquisite china, and large platters of food.

Amish women realize most of us would not choose their way for ourselves. They hope we discover a radiance in our own traditions and dare to yield to its light, whatever our customs may be. They hope we find time to create memories, not the kind found in photographs. They hope we listen to the voices that sing of tradition.

She Who Finds a Good Husband

Flesh of thy flesh, bone of thy bone,
I here, thou there, yet both but one.
—ANNE BRADSTREET,
"A Letter to Her Husband, Absent upon
Public Employment" (pub. 1678)

My people are completely patriarchal in their official congregational and family structure. Men call themselves heads of the household, adhering to a widely known Christian interpretation of men's and women's places in the home and community. Men serve as deacons and preachers and bishops. Women do not. Men are called leaders, women are not.

Many of us outside the Amish community embrace similar belief systems. Others of us cringe in the presence of these philosophies, wondering how any woman's experience can be fulfilling or healthy within such narrow boundaries. We observe these Amish women from afar, watching them move in and out of the spaces of modernity in their plain and simple garb, often with several children clinging close. We are certain this way of theirs could not be satisfying. This silence. This solemnity. This apparent lack of passion. We feel sorry for them.

Most Amish women I know do not feel sorry for themselves. While they give careful lip service to patriarchy, they experience, in actual practice, something much closer to mutuality. They seldom speak in official church settings but frequently give their opinions among friends and family members. They may not be heads of their homes, but they are often equal partners—women who know how to quietly, but firmly, make their wishes known and their voices heard.

I have heard many stories from women among my people who have influenced and even guided official decisions through their conversations with husbands and brothers and fathers and sons. I have also heard many stories about marriages of personal hopefulness and mutual trust.

These are women who admire and appreciate their partners. Who take pleasure in their husbands. Who cherish each of their children. Who know that happiness in marriage does not happen without work. Who foster peace and tranquillity, but who are also able to state their own needs for care and nurture.

These are women who are often passionate and seldom oppressed. Who revere but do not fear their husbands. Who respect the men in their lives and request the same in return. These are women who expect to be treated well. Who teach their daughters to do the same. Who believe that no woman should ever settle for anything less than a good husband.

Like my friend Mary, most Amish women are also convinced that submission and love are inseparably yoked. "It is much easier for me to submit because I know that he loves me." Submission cannot exist without love. That is what my people say. When both bless a marriage, the colors of the union become more vibrant, the shapes more interesting, and the movements more comforting.

Such possibility inspires each of us as we reach plateaus in our own less-than-perfect partnerships. We may view the concept of submission with far greater suspicion than most Amish women, but we can also acknowledge that in the presence of even proportions of respect and love, mutual surrender becomes an important ingredient of wellness. A goal worth pursuing with our husbands and partners.

Marriages and Soulmates

We also confess that there is in the church of God an honorable state of matrimony between two believers.

—*Dortrecht Confession of Faith*

"They say there's a soulmate for everyone." That's what my friend Eva told me one evening when we talked about marriage and meeting the right person. Like so many of my people, Eva thinks a great deal about the energy and work it takes to sustain a marriage. In her eyes, a woman should never settle for anyone less than her soulmate. She's right, I think.

We hope for the union of two souls. We desire someone who complements our family history, our life experiences, and our dreams. We look for a mate to lift us beyond ourselves and the limitations of our own worldview. Every once in a while, we meet that match early in life. In high school. Or even grade school, when we're very lucky.

For others it never seems to happen. We have reality to consider. People to fall in love with. Marriages to begin. We're often young, a little crazy, and very anxious not to be left behind in the search for fulfillment. *Bride's* magazine beckons. Parents worry. Friends have beautiful church weddings where everyone usually sounds and looks supremely happy. Why wait?

Young Amish women ask the same question. Most marry when they are very young, between eighteen and twenty-one. Too young, we sometimes think. Many appear innocent and untouched by some of the harder realities of living with another person and starting a family. This is why I find Eva's broad comment so intriguing, for I wonder how this waiting-for-the-right-person philosophy influences the choices women among my people make.

The Dortrecht Confession of Faith—the Amish church's written canon—contains a 250-word treatise with accompanying scriptures defining the sanctity of marriage. References to the solemn responsibility of establishing peaceful marriages surround and suffuse many elements of Amish women's lives. Teachers talk about it. Preachers preach about it. Parents try to set examples for their children. Young people read and receive instruction about marriage before they join the church. Very few Amish women or men enter into marriage lightly, having been repeatedly told their decision will stand for a lifetime.

Divorce and remarriage are not permitted. When irreconcilable differences separate two people, one or both usually leave the Amish community. Those who stay know they cannot remarry. This is the reason my people use words like "always" and "serious" when they speak of marriage.

I was sixteen with my first Amish boyfriend when my mother urged me not "to rush into anything." This union between two people, she said, was not something to entertain without thought. It should be considered with care. Because of the high view my people have of marriage, I know that many other young women receive similar advice from their mothers and aunts and grandmothers. Women like Eva.

LOUISE STOLTZFUS

❧ ❧

My people have no corner on these words of wisdom. Many of us have heard the same advice from our foremothers. We, too, believe in "a soulmate for everyone" and hope that our marriages last forever. But we also know this doesn't happen without solid commitments and the ability to live and let live. Nor does union with a soulmate guarantee success. In this hushed and holy undertaking, hope manifests itself in mutual surrender and forgiveness, in pleasantness and pleasure. Or so my people would say.

Marriage and Sexuality

Marriage should be honored by all, and the marriage bed kept pure.
—*Book of the Hebrews*

Many Amish women have a refreshing, but also very private, honesty about sexuality. A few find it difficult and even impossible to talk about, but most can smile and laugh with the best of us about the foibles and frustrations of love. They have well-defined opinions. Sexual union must be reserved for marriage. The world is much too permissive and quite decidedly out of control.

Evidence of the sad and painful effects of promiscuity, my people will go on to observe, increasingly burdens society. Teenage pregnancies. Abortions. Affairs. Broken homes. Divorces. All of which, in their view, are caused by a lack of respect for the sanctity of marriage, for the commitments necessary to make marriage work, and for the gift of sexual expression within marriage.

From the women who raised me, I learned that sexuality was a gift. A source of pleasure to be shared as part of the language of love in marriage. While some of us may argue with the narrowness of this interpretation, we cannot argue with its basic and fundamental goodness. Life and love have many dimensions. To corral these dimensions, as so much of popular culture does, into a one-dimensional and gratuitous depiction of sexuality seems to me, and to many of my people, a particular tragedy.

My people do believe society's overemphasis on sex is harmful, but they do not recommend denial of sexual expression as a solution. Vows of celibacy are not taken. Church leaders, those ordained to preach and teach, must be married. Amish women consider marriage a good and beautiful thing. Most desire it eagerly.

To the Amish, taking a vow of celibacy would only create a difficult reality, requiring a kind of discipline and rigor that does not interest them. They would rather come to easier terms, if they must, with not being married. While it is expected that those who do not marry remain celibate, most single women and men continue to express an openness to marriage and sometimes do so later in life. Other single people choose celibacy over marriage. Those few whose marriages break up are expected to remain celibate as long as they choose to stay Amish. Those who lose a partner to death may and often do remarry.

In the broad spaces outside the Amish reality, some of us, no doubt, disagree with my people and their views of sexuality and marriage. Others of us embrace their views, living as we do with similar moral and religious codes. My people make no apologies for a belief system that has sustained them through many generations. They will continue to share and teach their truth with great diligence. They will guide the young people growing up in their homes according to time-honored principles. They do not expect us to adopt their beliefs, but they hope we find equally honest, private, and secure ways to teach and share the encompassing beauty and wonder of physical expression in love and life.

LOUISE STOLTZFUS

❧ ❧

Bed Courtship and Bundling

Truly, a little love-making is a very pleasant thing.
—L. E. LANDON,
Romance and Reality (1831)

Young Amish women have the same curiosity about sex as young women everywhere. They giggle about it among themselves. They ask their mothers. As they grow older, they might have more serious conversations with each other, with a boyfriend, with a husband. Like women of every culture, some may never speak of this profoundly private experience, preferring to let whatever happens happen.

In many of their folkways, my people can only be called old-fashioned. They are, in fact, old-fashioned. While most of us have never heard of bed courtship and bundling, every young Amish woman will probably hear of this practice sometime in her life.

Since the eighteenth and nineteenth centuries, when bundling was more widely accepted among courting couples, little has been written about this rather harmless, warm, and exciting custom. Houses were cold in the evening. So, it is said, when a potential suitor came to see you, you invited him to your bed because it was the warmest and most private place in the house. Everyone understood that both partners remained fully clothed. Fully clothed? It sounds hopelessly old-fashioned and behind the times. Why would any young person today be interested?

Some Amish communities have retained this custom, in part, because they, too, do not have central heating systems, but also because it seems to them a better way for young people to explore the fires of passion than to have no restraints. Young men and women are both taught that sexual intercourse is not part of bundling. Young men learn to respect rather than pressure their partners.

LOUISE STOLTZFUS

❧ ❧

161

Perhaps bundling just happens to be an old-fashioned word for a very contemporary way of talking to our young people about passion and making love—which is why they might indeed be interested. As we talk with our teenagers about sexuality, most of us eventually realize that we can direct and guide, but we cannot control, behavior. We may find it wiser to suggest alternatives to the backseat of a car, to the pressures they may feel to "go all the way."

Most Amish women believe that the best way to guide a young person through the awakening of sexuality is to be honest and respectful. Influenced by scriptural teachings about abstinence, many also carefully instruct their young women and men not to engage in bed courtship. They plan with their daughters to keep living rooms and kitchens warm. They explain with thoughtful grace that the full expressions of physical love are reserved for marriage. Only after marriage should a young woman agree to become intimate. They tell their young men the same.

Whatever we believe about young people and love, we can surely understand that thoughtful and specific guidance, whether we teach abstinence or restraint, will be the best thing we can do for our young people. Those so loved and cared for are the ones most likely to find a whole and healthy way through the storms of youthful passion.

The Chemistry of Staying Together

I suspect that in every good marriage there are times when love seems to be over.
—MADELEINE L'ENGLE,
Two-Part Invention (1988)

My people believe mutual respect and similar interests are as important to a successful marriage as solid foundations and careful structures are to the longevity of a house. They talk and write with ease about these basic ingredients to the soundness of their community. They talk and write much less about romance, love, and sex.

Amish women have very little faith in the swept-off-your-feet, desperate physical attraction of two people in love. This, they say, nearly always cools quickly. My people put much more concern and energy into staying together through both hot and cold times than they put into getting together because of an intense sexual attraction.

It is a philosophy quite at odds with popular culture. Where pop culture asks, "Did I feel giddy and electric?" Amish women ask, "Did I feel interested and comfortable?" Where pop culture declares, "Sleep together, go all the way, make love," Amish women suggest, "Serve him food because the way to a man's heart is through his stomach." Where pop culture says, "I will always love you (even if you don't love me)," Amish women say, "I like you. I respect you. I will do my best to be content with you always."

Those of us immersed in television and film are hard-pressed to escape the subtle influences this medium projects into theaters and living rooms. We are caught up in a certain preoccupation with romance and sex. We might find the Amish way backward and provincial.

We might also find it inspiring. For we will surely find ourselves in cold relationships, even those that have been hot for a long time. We may discover the person we love is someone we don't like, especially in a moment of disagreement. We may find ourselves uncomfortable and bored. We may be tempted to run.

My people maintain that the hope of permanent union rests in the ability to move beyond the light-headed chemistry of physical attraction to the more even chemistry of emotional and intellectual attraction. And they recommend that such chemistry be discovered before marriage. Amish women also believe these connections are found in talking about more than love. In recognizing that a life together involves both pleasure and pain. In working throughout the marriage on the symmetry between challenging each other's intellect and worldview and relaxing in the easy spaces of each other's comfort and sameness.

Although my people usually call this commitment rather than chemistry, they are sure it is the source of real hope and happiness in relationships and marriages. They think it has much more to do with what we believe than it has to do with our inclination to glibly tell our partners "I love you." Love alone, they say, cannot sustain a marriage. Just as a foundation needs a structure before it can be called a home, so a marriage needs interest and respect before it can be called a union of love.

It has always seemed to me that my people have latched onto a primal truth about human nature and the emotions coupled with romance. While their experiences with love and marriage are surely as varied as women of any community, they enter into a partnership because they are committed to staying together for life, not because they feel an insatiable physical attraction, though the attraction is certainly also an element in the union. We who are not Amish will doubtless find it much easier to stay together when we do the same.

Fasting, Feasting, and Holidays

We rested again and again.
—DOROTHY WORDSWORTH,
The Grasmere Journals (1802)

Like many of us, Amish women look forward to the rest and celebration of holidays. My people commemorate most of the traditional Christian holidays—Easter, Thanksgiving, Christmas, and New Year's Day. But the Easter season is the height of leisure in the Amish community. Everyone tries to take time off on six different days during this time of the year: Good Friday. Easter Sunday. Easter Monday. Pentecost Sunday. Pentecost Monday. And Ascension Day.

My people approach this special season of Easter and early spring with the same reserve and seriousness that mark their entire understanding of faith. Neither Easter bunnies nor fine new outfits fit their belief that the death of Jesus was a solemn moment in history, a moment they wish to remember with silence, fasting, and personal reflection.

Although they forgo the finery of the season for silence and fasting, my people also respond to the hopeful messages of spring and new life with long, happy hours of visiting and feasting. Good Friday begins with quiet reflection. Children read and relax. Adults fast throughout the morning, reading the Bible and meditating.

The tempo of the day usually quickens with a simple, but satisfying, noon meal. In the afternoon, children play games and adults join in, glad for a break from the everyday work and wear of life.

Easter Monday and Pentecost Monday typically are days to host large gatherings complete with ham and turkey dinners with all the trimmings. Old family recipes for stuffing, scalloped potatoes, or pineapple sauce appear as everyone joins in to help make the meal.

Uncles and aunts tell stories. Cousins reconnect. Grandparents smile as they rest in the nurture of their many children and grand-children.

For everyone—young and old alike—the spring holidays are a wel-come respite in a busy time. Throughout the spring, women must concentrate on raking and mowing lawns, cleaning houses from top to bottom, and plowing and planting fields and gardens. My people find that synchronizing days of fasting and feasting with days of work keeps them well and happy during this time. Their spring holiday traditions reveal a surprising balance of work, rest, and play at the soul of Amish philosophy.

It is a balance we might all seek to achieve regardless of our reli-gious or secular traditions. Fasting renews the spirit, feasting renews the body. Both have restorative value. Both keep us from drowning in the drudgery of endless cycles of work. Both are worth considering as we search for meaning and wellness in days filled with activity and movement.

Why not set aside a Good Friday or Easter Monday in our own tradition? Why not turn off all the stereos, computers, and televisions for one morning of each spring? Why not take the time for contem-plation and reflection? Why not prepare a feast—large or small? Why not declare the preparation and partaking of a family dinner a time for gathering and making memories? Perhaps in the pursuit of these simple pleasures, we will discover renewed appreciation for holidays, remembering that these special times are meant to be about relaxation and rest.

Playing Mary and the Meaning of Christmas

To us a Child of hope is born
To us a Son is given.
—JOHN MORISON,
Scottish Paraphrases (1781)

*T*here's an encompassing beauty about it, the holiday season. From the breathless excitement of small children to the more restrained communion of families baking cookies and cakes, the weeks leading up to December 25 each year fill our senses with cinnamon and cider, ceremony and celebration. It's a time of togetherness many of us would not want to miss. We pull out the decorations, revisit traditions, and make plans to receive guests, attend carol singings or candlelighting events, and immerse ourselves in the joys of the time.

There's also an almost frantic madness about it. The retailers hawking "a good season" spawn scrooges grumping about "Christmas music in the stores already" as early as November 1. Wish lists and shopping lists grow as the malls and centers of commerce adopt an air of festivity laden with decorated trees, greenery, poinsettias, and presents. Commercial messages seem to bombard our every waking hour.

That is where my people draw a line. "We feel Christmas has become much too commercial" is a common refrain among Amish women. In the Amish tradition, Christmas revolves around memory and family gatherings. Memory of the birth of Jesus. Memory of the coming of a child of hope. Memory of the consuming goodness of the Christmas message.

Their one-room country schools often have annual Christmas programs, but they work hard to focus on songs, poems, and occasional skits that recount, as they say, "the real meaning of Christmas." Santa Claus, excessive decorations, and Christmas trees usually do not find their way into Amish schools or homes.

Emma describes Christmas morning with her family of five: "We try to keep it simple. I might bring in a few greens and light a candle on the table. Each of our children gets one gift, and John reads the Christmas story from the Bible. By the time we have breakfast, it's time to pack everybody up and head to *Dawdy*'s [Grandpa's] for our family Christmas dinner. The children always look forward to playing with their cousins."

All of us have different holiday customs, but we may want to consider at least a portion of the Amish way. The simplicity and reverence with which my people approach this season beckon us to scale down, especially when the merrymaking becomes a nightmare of work and chaos, of racing from place to place in search of the latest Cabbage Patch, Barbie, or Elmo. Children love this time of the year because of its warmth and energy. With a bit of gentle persuasion, they will often willingly join in easier celebrations and quieter visions of sugar plums and fairies.

Two years ago my extended family, which has grown to include forty-five people, realized that purchasing gifts for each other had become more burdensome than anything else. We heard ourselves groaning repeatedly, "I don't know what she needs or wants." One of my very wise sisters suggested substituting the afternoon gift exchange with an impromptu program and a Christmas pageant featuring the children.

As family members began arriving in the days before Christmas, several of us coordinated on-the-spot costumes (involving lots of pliable cardboard, yarn, blankets, and bedsheets). We held one rehearsal in an upstairs bedroom on Christmas morning. The children were absolutely giddy with delight, and my six-year-old niece, who played Mary, will probably never forget. Would she have remembered several dozen gifts? In our family lore, that Christmas is quickly becoming "one of our best ever." It was also a wonderful evocation of our Amish heritage and its high regard for commemorating the true meaning of the season.

Artists and Dreamers

I've dreamt in my life dreams that have stayed with me ever after, and changed my ideas: they've gone through and through me, like wine through water, and altered the color of my mind.
—EMILY BRONTË,
Wuthering Heights (1847)

Few Amish women consider themselves artists, but many are dreamers. They are like women everywhere who dream of people, places, and things they may never know. The fervor and zest of an Amish woman's dreams are often directed and given to sewing beautiful quilts rather than painting landscapes with oil and watercolor, making colorful desserts rather than creating exquisite dishes in gourmet restaurants, or tending pleasing flower gardens rather than visiting galleries and museums. These quilts, desserts, and gardens are expressions of everyday pleasantness and usefulness. They bring a sense of satisfaction to the dreamers and artists among my people.

For even in Amish circles, an artist is someone who makes art for art's sake. She paints, composes, or writes because she cannot help herself, not because she wants to make something useful or beautiful. And making art because you have to, because you feel good only when you do, is a way of life few Amish women can fathom. It seems to them a waste of time. A source of distance from others in the community. A first step down the road to not being Amish.

The alienation Amish women artists consequently live with comes not only from my people and their interpretation of the creative process, but also from the world and its prejudices. Many young artists have heard their parents say, "But you'll have to find a way to make a living." Many struggling artists have proven their parents correct. And many successful artists have found themselves subjects of the refrain "That's just how artists are—a little different, a little weird."

Artists know this. Creative energy is a humbling force. It can bring cool, welcome relief from the heat and passion of thoughts, actions, and behaviors, but it can also move through the mind and body with the destructive power of a tornado or hurricane. It can be isolating and lonely. It is rarely desired in tightly knit communities where imagination must necessarily yield at times to what others cannot accept.

My friend Martha doesn't let herself think too much about it. She paints because she feels better as one feels better after exercise or sleep or food. She paints because she cannot wait to see what the strokes of her hand will do to the paper. She paints because after fifteen minutes with a brush and watercolors, she has renewed strength to face the other challenges of being a wife and mother.

She is an artist, and she knows it. What other people think or say about her self-knowledge sometimes gives her pause. Most times, though, she succeeds in following her heart. A heart that wants to paint, wants to be Amish, and wants to be an artist.

Whatever is incongruous about her heart's desire has its theme in many of our stories—artists who produce work our people, whoever they may be, cannot accept or understand. We compose, paint, and write what we know—our truth—and hope our people will understand or at least look the other way. When criticism comes, we are sometimes devastated, sometimes chagrined, sometimes outraged, and sometimes sorry.

Like Martha we must go on. For it is only in moving on that anyone grows. Whether or not we are members of close and sheltered groups like the Amish, we will continue to make art if we care about our dreams. It is the nature of the creative process.

Amish Woman Makes Good

General rules are dangerous of application in particular instances.

—CHARLOTTE H. YONGE,
The Pillars of the House, vol. 2 (1889)

They are questions most women wonder about at some time: Could I support this family? Could I support myself? Among the Amish, home life turns on the belief that women shall be mothers and homemakers, whereas men shall be fathers and breadwinners. However, my people also allow for variations on this common theme. Not all women want to be mothers and homemakers. Not all men want to be fathers and breadwinners. Sometimes to hold the script together, the drama needs a new character. Such has been the case with Amish women and small businesses.

In the 1960s when our neighbor opened a small fabric shop in the front room of her home, none of us imagined her on the leading edge of a growing phenomenon—Amish women running their own businesses. My parents described her situation with simple straightforwardness, "She needs to make a living," and we frequented her store. Most of the dresses my sisters and I wore through the years came from fabric purchased in Susie's store.

We understood. It was about survival. Without her courage, her family would have faced an ongoing struggle with poverty. Because of her flair for business and finance, she became the family breadwinner, lifting a great burden from her husband's shoulders. Hers is a quintessential story of breaking rules to make a partnership work.

In humble country churches and bustling city cathedrals, the melodrama of traditional roles for women and men will probably always be performed. We have heard the words—"If women would stay home where they belong, we would have fewer juvenile delinquents" or "If men would only do their part in taking leadership at home, children would have fewer problems."

Why not let the playwrights edit the script? "If men and women will use their strengths to balance their union, they and their children will be happier." Or, "If men and women will work together to support each other, they and their children will be more whole."

Susie took such a risk, and her people accepted the decision. They did not let rigidity cloud their view of reality. They were right. She made good. Her small fabric shop grew into a large dry-goods and sewing supply store. She remains a humble Amish woman, at peace with herself and her husband.

As an Amish woman entrepreneur, she is also no longer alone. Many women among my people have become proprietors of prosperous small businesses—greenhouses, bookstores, quilt shops, and bakeries—sharing with the men in their lives the burdens of putting food on the table and clothes in the closet. They are, like many of us, using the combined strengths of partnership to balance family life.

Some women are much better financial planners and checkbook balancers than their husbands. Some men are much better cooks and childcare providers than their wives. Making adjustments in family roles may be risky, but the tired themes we women of the world have become accustomed to must never keep us from reaching together for the rewards of shared strengths and divided weaknesses. Many of my people have quietly discovered this. May we do the same.

Should I
Hire a Maid?

People can say what they like about the eternal verities, love and truth and so on, but nothing's as eternal as the dishes.

—MARGARET MAHY,
The Catalogue of the Universe (1995)

*A*s women, we have many different opinions about domesticity and how to balance its repetitions with our working lives. A few of us labor all day and far into the evening. Some of us let the house go and live with dirt and dust. Many of us enlist the services of partners and children. Whatever our strategies for dealing with this never-ending responsibility, we are often weary of grit and grime, tired of cooking, and exhausted by the expectations so exquisitely positioned on our shoulders.

Women among my people know of no easy regimen for holding an even keel in these times. Their problems may not be about receipts not matching cash-register tapes, company meetings conflicting with school activities, bosses firmly requesting longer hours in a deadline crunch, or dozens of customers requiring equal attention. But the demands of six or seven young children, a large family farm, and a pile of dirty laundry exact of them the same level of sanity and stamina. They understand strain and stress. And they look for solutions.

When one of my sisters-in-law, who is not Amish, acknowledged feelings of inadequacy around her decision to hire another woman to clean their house, my mother surprised her by saying, "I always had a hired girl when the children were little."

So she did. I remember a succession of young women who helped clean the house, fold the laundry, weed the garden, and care for the newest baby. Their presence freed our mother from the all-consuming claims of domestic life. She was a better woman and a better mother. Even today she says, "It was a good investment."

My parents were not unusual. They were young with lots of small children, and they hired a maid. It was about achieving a sense of balance, a bearable load. Many young Amish mothers do likewise. Grateful for burdens lifted, they enjoy the companionship of the teenage Amish women available to them, young people glad for the extra dollars they can make working for someone else.

Like the decision my people make to have lots of children, we all make choices that multiply the stresses in our lives. We have high-pressure careers. Husbands. Children. Aging parents. All of whom require our attention and focus. We hope to make a difference. We want to be good citizens so we say yes to requests for volunteers in our churches, schools, and neighborhood centers.

Because we cannot be superwomen, we must necessarily make

some concessions and sacrifices. Maybe we quit our jobs and live more simply. Maybe we hire domestic help and come home to delightfully clean houses on occasion. Maybe we accept some clutter and chaos. Whatever we do to offset the strain and stress, the busy whirl of our homes, Amish women like my mother are likely to tell us, "I've done the same thing."

View from a Buggy

Two roads diverged in a wood, and I—
I took the one less traveled by,
And that has made all the difference.
—ROBERT FROST,
"The Road Not Taken" (1915)

*T*here are many ways to alter perspective. To approach both our physical and spiritual realities, at least for a short time, from a different angle. Sometimes a change of scenery helps. Which is why we look forward to holidays and vacations. Sometimes a change of environment helps. Which is why we rearrange furniture and file drawers or buy plants and fresh-cut flowers. Sometimes a change of life helps. Which is why we choose a different religious persuasion, vocation, or even partner. All of this movement—some of it routine and some of it radical—is about perspective. About the view from the kitchen window. The view from the corner office. Or the view from the Jeep Cherokee.

View and perspective interest Amish women. They are often quick to assert their almost universal belief that we, the women of the world, move too fast. "Why are you always in such a rush? I would think this running from place to place would soon wear you out." They are also quick to blame our Jeep Cherokees, our Audis and Hondas and Saturns. "We don't want cars because we see how much they change family life."

The absence of convenient public transportation does not permit most of us to choose the Amish way. We are not Amish. We need our cars. We don't want the problem of hiring Amish taxis (as the folks who provide private auto transportation for the Amish are called) whenever we wish to go somewhere farther or more quickly than a buggy can take us. We like the convenience of our cars.

My people approach this subject from the opposite side. They like the *inconvenience* of their buggies. The view from a buggy keeps them closer to the earth, closer to the rhythms of their rural reality. It lets them take the road less traveled.

Amish women rarely envy us our cars. They have seen our teen-agers speeding down the highways. They have heard us lament our few opportunities to gather the whole family for an evening meal. They have heard us tell of racing to soccer practices, piano lessons, and all of the other betterment projects we offer ourselves and our children. The automobile, many Amish women maintain, has forever changed the way families interact.

Though few of us will join the Amish in their resolve, we can, on occasion, change our view. Why not slow down? Why not choose backroads instead of freeways? Why not drive forty miles an hour instead of seventy? Why not say no to a few more of the many requests that demand we hit the roads and rails? Why not spend more time at home with our children? Indeed, why not treat ourselves to a ride in a buggy?

Amish women would agree that a moonlight carriage ride through Central Park, a midday surrey around the French Quarter, or an early evening buggy ride through their own quiet countryside changes perspective. All awaken a certain expectation of romance and intrigue. Of enchantment and wonder. All offer, though they may be fleeting, an opportunity to view the landscape of our lives differently. Each will help us remember details—the shimmering moonlit trees, the fanciful ironwork, or the uncommon fragrance of summertime honeysuckle. Each will lull the senses and slow the pace of emotions drained by movement and the rapid buzz of our highways and homes.

The Accumulation of Wealth: Friend or Foe?

Enough is as good as a feast.
—KATHERINE TYNAN,
The Years of Shadow (1919)

Money can be a friend. When we have enough, life is good. We can buy food, cars that run efficiently, occasional brand-name clothing for our children, and homes with furniture and plants, paintings and photos. We are happy.

Money can also be an enemy. When we have too much or too little, an obsession with its power often controls our thoughts, our conscious and subconscious lives. We are not happy.

How do we, therefore, understand the concept of enough money? How do we live within our means? These questions intrigue many Amish women. Living, as they do, in a society that places little value on material goods or the accumulation of wealth, my people engage in a constant dialogue over personal accountability regarding matters of finance. "The church definitely frowns on the appearance of wealth. Those who have lots of money know better than to flaunt it." Rachel is expressing her clear opinions about money. "I think you have to know when enough is enough. You don't need to be rich to be happy."

Because my people are not communal and every family manages its own finances, some individuals do become wealthy. The church has no written guidelines regarding the use of money, but it does have many spoken taboos against hoarding resources and coveting riches. Those who defy the common wisdom with extravagant living generally find themselves a few steps outside the good graces of the community. Those who avoid the appearance of wealth by living frugally and giving freely to others in need find themselves revered and honored by their neighbors and friends. "They have plenty of money, but they are such generous people" is a high compliment reserved for people whose actions demonstrate an understanding of the church's views about money.

The opposite problem of too little money creates a different predicament for my people. Through gentle, and sometimes not so gentle, persuasion and peer pressure, families are urged to live within their means. Those few who acquire debt beyond their control usually turn to the church for help. When the debt is caused by loss of a job, illness, or some other emergency, the community pitches in with great generosity of spirit. When the debt is perceived to result from poor management or wastefulness, my people are less likely to give money and more likely to give lots of free advice about living more frugally and carefully. Among my people, the balancing act required to walk the tightrope of enough money presents many challenges.

LOUISE STOLTZFUS

❧ ❧

It is the same for all of us. When we are stressed out with unmanageable debt, we are most wise when we turn somewhere for help. If we cannot choose the church, perhaps we can turn to family members or consumer-credit counseling agencies. As we rescue ourselves from the ruin and pain of debt, we, too, will find freedom as we begin to accept and understand the concept of having enough money.

When we have too much money, we might also consider the Amish way. Perhaps, we will choose not to purchase second homes or go on long resort vacations and, instead, make significant contributions to the world's many needy and deserving causes. In so doing, we will free ourselves of the destruction and greed that so often accompany too much money.

The Psychology of Common Sense

*I*t's what you learn after you know it all that counts.
—JUDITH KELMAN,
Someone's Watching (1991)

*W*hat is common sense? Simple wisdom from simple folk. Ordinary good sense and sound practical judgment. An inner light directing our thoughts, decisions, and lifeways. The high guide of the psyche providing balance and parameters for all of our actions and reactions.

This is what I learned about common sense from the Amish women and men who surrounded me as a child and young person. "Simple wisdom" and "sound practical judgment" were easy-to-understand ideas communicated by proclamation. "An inner light" and the "high guide of the psyche" were more complicated thought processes that my people transmitted by osmosis.

These were, after all, plain-spoken, humble people who expressed enormous confidence in simplicity and mutual intelligence. "Use your common sense" was often-repeated counsel from both of my parents. It worked for deciding whether I should wear boots in the snow, whether I should try climbing to the peak of the barn, whether or not I could defy the laws of nature or gravity. It also worked for deciding how to treat others, how to react when I was injured or hurt, and how to express my needs and desires.

If I followed the simple wisdom of common sense, I would not be led astray. That was the unspoken rule behind my parents' desire that I call upon and rely on my inner light. A latter-day parent might say, "I trust you to make your own decisions." The meaning is the same.

"Common sense." It is a phrase that echoes across the canyons of our memories, catching the melodic tones of ordinary people imparting age-old wisdom. It is a phrase that reveals at its well-worn depth wide and deep rivers of wellness and strength. It is a phrase to hold and pass on to future generations.

Most Amish women believe the source of internal wisdom to be the spirit of God. They place little confidence in the study of the psyche or in attempts to analyze the vast complexities of the human mind. They prefer pouring out their problems to trusted sisters and friends and seldom understand the value of weekly visits to a stranger for therapy. Common sense tells them healing happens within the gathered community.

My friend Rachel adds an amendment to her introspective evaluation of common sense and the study of the mind: "There are difficult times. Times when people need to go see a counselor. We don't stand in the way. Most of us believe when you can't cope, you need to seek professional help."

I realized how completely my Amish upbringing guides my worldview when I discovered myself agreeing with everything Rachel said. The pop psychology of seeing a therapist makes little sense to those of us raised on heavy doses of common sense. While we do not deny the worth of those arts whose disciplines include healing the mind, we hate the thought of losing communities committed to free caregiving and counseling. We depend on friendships and sisterhood. Mothers listening to daughters. And daughters listening to mothers.

We understand limited resources and heavy burdens, but we cannot accept the suggestion that every disturbance of the psyche needs a trained and paid professional. Common sense tells us to be more willing to listen, to extend a hand of friendship for the down cycles of our everyday hardships and sorrows. To be there for each other.

The Paradox of Heaviness and Lightness

> *I* learned to make my mind large, as the universe is large, so that there is room for paradoxes.
> —MAXINE HONG KINGSTON,
> *The Woman Warrior (1976)*

*I*t was a photograph that caught my eye. An old Amish woman bent at the waist with hands to the ground, retrieving leftover ears of corn after a horse-drawn picker had passed through the field. Her garb, which covered every inch of her body, was completely black. Her face was hidden behind the sides of a plain, dark bonnet. I couldn't even see her hands, covered with gloves against the rough corn and cold autumn day. From the limits of my two-dimensional view, her life appeared to be one of hardship and suffering, one of heaviness and misery.

It was a photograph that caught my eye. A twenty-something Amish mother, standing inside her home with face turned in profile to the camera. She held a child whose angelic twinkle seemed to sing out, "I am well loved." The mother gazed openly and kindly, smiling at her daughter and taking part in a friendly conversation with the photographer. Again from the limits of my two-dimensional view, her life appeared to be one of gaiety and pleasure, one of lightness and joy.

While each is an accurate depiction of Amish women's lives, neither photograph gives a true rendering of their individual stories, much less the whole of Amish women's experiences. From the images left by the first photograph, we postmodern women might be inclined to run from the Amish way. From the images in the second, we might be inclined to run toward it. Neither response is especially helpful. To Amish women or to us.

In truth most women among my people have an abundance of

both heaviness and lightness in their days. They sob during funeral services. And perhaps smile quickly over a funny story told later that day at the funeral meal. They giggle at weddings. And cry at the thought of sons and daughters having grown up so fast. They bend beneath the burdens of hard work. And rise with gladness for each new morning.

From the women who raised me, I learned that one of the more precarious of life's balancing acts, but also one of the most important, was the weight between heaviness and lightness. My grandmothers, aunts, and my mother told their stories. They thought it especially tragic when darkness overcame a person, but they also lived with, as they called it, an attitude of seriousness.

As we face the somber, broken images of our own realities, may we find the courage to turn toward the sun and warmth of hopefulness. May we also find the strengh to rise from the cornfields and go home, thankful for the harvest. May we have the grace to both smile and cry at funerals and sob and laugh at weddings, embracing these paradoxes of human experience with a great bear hug of care and compassion.

LOUISE STOLTZFUS

❀ ❀

We Have
Respect for the Dying

Death be not proud, though some have called thee
Mighty and dreadful, for thou art not so.
——JOHN DONNE,
Holy Sonnets (1633)

Some of us do not believe in dying. One Amish friend told me the story of her nephew. After leaving the Amish community as a young adult, he married and joined a charismatic Christian fellowship with an absolute belief in the miraculous gifts of divine healing. The young man developed a life-threatening illness.

True to form, his church community took up a call of prayer for healing. His sickness was denied. He was encouraged not to yield to it. Others, including Amish family members, were admonished to have more faith because any lack of faith would hinder the power of God, prevent the young man from experiencing a miracle, and keep him from becoming well. Even when he was taken to a hospital in the final weeks of his life, the church held on to its call for a miracle. He died.

I thought this story was an altered and more extreme version of the way many of us approach the process of dying. We deny it. We do our utmost to stay young forever. We seek every form of treatment for catastrophic illness we can find. We find it difficult, if not impossible, to surrender our loved ones, to walk peacefully and lovingly beside them through the hard steps of dying.

My friend ended her sad story in tears, "At least there is one thing I can say for the Amish. We have respect for the dying." I cannot stop thinking about what she meant. I remembered words I've heard my father pray countless times, "If it is your will, make her [or him] well. But if not, than give her rest. And release her to full healing."

LOUISE STOLTZFUS

By full healing, he means death. This prayer, so characteristic of my people, expresses a central Amish understanding. They do not wish someone to stay here in pain and suffering when the person will find rest in a much better place.

My people generally have no desire to prolong life. When death is inevitable, they want to know, and they want to take their family members home. To care for them in familiar places, to alleviate their suffering as much as possible, and to be close to them through what might otherwise be a dark and lonely journey.

Surrendering ourselves to the process of death and knowing when extraordinary measures only extend suffering are difficult life learnings. Sometimes we cannot let go because it may mean our loved ones will stop fighting to stay with us. The Amish, too, struggle with these questions.

Most, like my friend, have little sympathy with those who call for divine miracles, who deny the value of treatment. My people support, as do most of us, medical intervention against disease and its ravages. But they have a precedence for knowing when enough is enough. Time after time, they turn to their God and pray for strength to give up, to let the suffering one go.

To Amish women, yielding is part of a holistic approach to dying, a respect for both the person and the process. My people believe in giving dignity to the process of dying. They understand that the cycle of life includes both birth and death. And they have little desire to deny the power of either.

My Cousin's Son

Where, O death, is your victory?
Where, O death, is your sting?
—*First Book of the Corinthians*

On a cold, late fall afternoon about ten years ago, my cousin's six-year-old son was hit by a car on his way home from the one-room country school near their farm. He died. The youngest child, he was much loved by his parents and older brothers and sisters. Their grief over an unexpected and unavoidable tragedy was as palpable as the first bitter winds of autumn. The neighborhood and community quickly gathered around them.

I attended the visitation, or viewing (as my people say). Held in the family home and guided by a local funeral director, viewings are open to anyone. Funerals, on the other hand, are by invitation only. The Amish attend funerals when they "receive word" from a representative of the family, and they generally expect the same of those friends and family members who are not Amish.

Responses to the death of a loved one vary widely among cultures. Jewish families gather to say *kaddish*, the mourner's prayer. African villagers prepare for weeks, conducting all-night wakes and three-day funerals after hundreds of mourners arrive from distant places. Mennonites have huge church funerals with long lines filing by the coffin.

My people visit each other. They are glad and pleased when others come by to share support and sorrow for their loss—when they come to the viewing but also to their home for weeks and months following the death. "We need to go see Dan and Sue on Sunday afternoon" or "Don't you think we should visit Uncle John and Aunt Rachel again?" is the way my dad prefaces his comments to my mother about those on whom they need to call.

As important to this culture as going to church, Sunday visits also demonstrate care and concern for other life-changing events—marriage, the birth of a child, or a move to a new home. While we may envy this custom or wish, as I do, to be better practitioners, my friend Elizabeth thinks her people also have much to learn from others about helpful responses to grief.

After the accidental death of her own son, she found herself reaching beyond the familiar customs and rituals of her Amish world. "Yes, our friends came to visit us, but so many found it hard to talk about our son. They talked about the weather, the crops, and everything else. I just wanted them to say his name."

Elizabeth read everything she could find about grief and coping with loss. She wrote a book about her experiences and began, with her husband, to carry messages of healing and hope to her people. "So many times people think they don't want to remind you of the one who has died. It's not reminding, because you're already thinking about it. You can't stop thinking about it."

Few of us feel comfortable in the face of grief, but Elizabeth's words, it seems to me, illustrate the importance of simply being gentle and present and thoughtful. I will never forget the bright tears in my cousin's eyes as she stood beside her son surrounded by those who cared for her. People who had come to share her grief.

The Soothing Sounds of Silence

In quietness and in confidence shall be your
strength.

—Book of Isaiah

Most Amish women do not desire silence, the absence of any sound or noise, but they long to find quietness, the soothing sounds of silence. Silent retreats, like those sponsored by monasteries and other centers for thought, generally do not appeal to women among my people. They have a great love for song and conversation—the sound advice of an older woman, the comforting murmur of a mother's voice, the spoken words of a preacher, the deep, rich chant of an ancient German hymn. They sit with willing quietness through hour-long sermons, preferring the droning tones of a preacher to silent Quaker meetings.

They are not silent women, but they are quiet women. Because they often live far from the din of commerce, factories, and traffic, my people may have an advantage in the search for calm and quiet places for the soul. But most of these women maintain that quietness is not so much about the exterior location of our homes as it is about what we do inside them.

When we bring harsh words, loud music, and the constant buzzing and beeping of microwave ovens, TVs, telephones, and computers into our homes, they say, we will have less quietness. Amish women work hard to keep these sounds from overtaking the interior spaces of their homes. They do not always succeed, but many of their homes are indeed places of quietness, filled with the calm sounds of silence.

My people preach and teach that homes are meant to be havens of rest. Places where people who live together respect each other's right to live in peace, not without discussion or disagreement but without the polarizing differences of those who refuse to give and take. This is no small task. Especially in large families with children of many ages. But parents and children strive to discover quietness, to envelop their homes with the sounds of silence. "We like our long, winter evenings; the children all sitting around reading or playing games. Sometimes they get a little noisy, but that's all part of family life."

Amish women faithfully protect the sanctity of their homes by rejecting the chief noisemakers that have found their way into most of ours. They hope we, too, will find ways to create the sounds of silence. To find in our homes a quiet haven from the clamor and noise of society. To fill them with silent spaces, private sanctuaries, and relaxing camaraderie.

For many of us, this is a difficult task. We long to come home to tranquillity only to be interrupted by the telephone. We hope for a moment of silence, but the stereo system (perhaps in a neighbor's car) pounds out its disturbing beat. We wish to sit still for a while, but we're only minutes from the beginning of a favorite TV program.

How, then, do we make our homes havens of rest? To women among my people, the answers are obvious. Like them, we make some careful resolutions. We unplug our telephones occasionally. We become involved in our communities and work together to lower the levels of sound outside our homes. We spend at least one evening a week with books and games, the TV turned off. We tune in to the sounds of silence.

Drop by Anytime

Sharing is sometimes more demanding than giving.
—MARY CATHERINE BATESON,
Composing a Life (1989)

There are several ways to turn our homes into havens of rest. One is to close the doors and make them places to escape the world, to escape other people. Another is to open the doors, to like them so well we want to share them. Many Amish women subscribe to the second way. They keep homes where friends and family members feel welcome anytime.

"Drop by anytime." Amish women say these three simple words to each other all the time. Sharing and visiting help them to solve problems. Front-porch conversations ease the dissonance of differences among people. Open doors reinforce their connections and ties to each other. They love to share knowledge, food, spaces, life. I am often surprised by their genuine openness to an interruption, by their ability to mold the interruption into the regular movements of tasks they want or need to complete. Many times they've asked me to come in and continued to cook, sew, or plant a garden, inviting me to help or move around them as we talk. Other times they drop whatever they've been doing, kick up their heels, bring out a cup of tea or coffee, and sit back to revel in a chance to visit and relax.

One early spring evening I made careful plans to spend time with both Eva and Rachel. When I came to Eva's home, she suggested we drive over to Rachel's. Concerned because Rachel wasn't expecting me until several hours later, I hesitated.

"Oh, it's fine. She won't mind." And of course Eva was right. In the midst of a sewing project, Rachel immediately and gladly dropped what she was doing and spent the next three hours visiting. The sewing could wait until tomorrow.

I have moved so far from this ideal of my childhood. In my search for individual success and freedom, I have lost the ability to keep my doors open. My words are nearly always "Call me before you come." Not because I don't like people, but because I don't want to be interrupted in the pursuit of escape and relaxation.

Somewhere between "Drop by anytime" and "Call me before you come" might be the place to begin. Why not sit on the front-porch swing to read the paper? Why not visit with the neighbors? Why not spend fewer hours on escape and more on connections? For women among my people, these are the common exercises of community life. Their homes are extensions of the community, places to share and come together.

To shift from home as haven of escape to home as haven in community stretches many of us beyond our comfort zones. We may not wish to do it often, but we may be blessed for doing it sometimes. The first small steps may be filled with failure, especially when we live in culturally diverse neighborhoods or the commonplace isolation of suburbia. But we may also discover the deeper level of peace and safety that comes from knowing and appreciating our neighbors. From sharing front-porch-stoop and across-the-fence conversations.

May we each have the tiny successes that underscore the value of trying. A neighborhood child smiling as she walks by, "Your flowers are so pretty." A pleasant conversation with friends as twilight falls. A cold morning of shoveling snow, followed, perhaps, by the shared warmth of soup and hot chocolate.

Competition
or Cooperation

Cooperation is an intelligent functioning of the concept of laissez faire—a thorough conviction that nobody can get there unless everybody gets there.
—VIRGINIA BURDEN TOWER,
The Process of Intuition (1975)

Competition. For jobs. For status. For men. As women of the world, we yield ourselves too freely to an uncontrolled cycle of competition. With men, sometimes. With other women, much more often.

What drives us to succeed often also drives us to compete. We close the doors to each other's stories to preserve an edge. As waitresses, teachers, editors, or lawyers, we feel pressed to protect our turf. To secure our jobs. To capture and keep our partners.

What begins as friendly suspicion in high school corridors often accelerates into outright hostility when we enter the workplace. "You stay away from my man" turns into "I will do whatever it takes to make sure you stay in your place, to be certain you do not threaten my job security." Why do we do this? That is the question Amish women wonder about.

"Why do you do this?"

Cooperation and the free sharing of information are central themes in many Amish women's lives. "You don't need to put another person down just to get ahead yourself. That's the best way not to get ahead!" is how I've heard my people explain their theory about friendship and competition.

LOUISE STOLTZFUS

❀ ❀

They seldom understand the drive to keep one foot up on the person next to us. The need to win at any cost. The secrecy that so often fosters the competitive spirit in our places of work. Why, they ask, do we close so many doors among women because of competition? Why not give more energy to cooperation?

Usually, they mean sharing stories and friendship, recipes and patterns, quilting designs and springtime seeds. Sometimes, though, they go even further. They also mean supporting a friend's chance to make a living, even when it may directly affect what they do. It is not uncommon for one Amish quilt shop owner, when asked, to freely direct a potential customer to a competitor down the road.

Many of us have an immediate reaction. That's okay for Amish women, but not for me. Until we stop and think. What if the school where you teach is so infested with competition and lack of cooperation that students actually receive inferior educations? Would it not be wiser to help a newcomer understand some of the techniques of controlling a classroom rather than being driven by the fear of losing a rung on the ladder of success? What if the diner where you wait tables gives you heartburn because of rampant competition and lack of cooperation? Would it not be wiser to offer an occasional helping hand to a struggling fellow server, giving kindness a chance and making your own life less stressful? My people are very certain the answers to these questions are a resounding chorus of yeses.

That is not to say Amish women have no sense of competition, no reasons to protect their own spaces or ways of making a living. However, because of their high regard for cooperation, most are quick to note that "not giving away the business secrets" does not necessarily translate to cutthroat competition. They are committed to the free sharing of ideas because it benefits community life, opening the gates to gathered stories and mutual friendships. I think they are wiser and richer for it. We might strive for the same balance in our own worlds.

Flavor and Flair
of My Mother's Kitchen

*F*ood imaginatively and lovingly prepared, and eaten in good company, warms the being.
—MARJORIE KINNAN RAWLINGS,
Cross Creek Cookery (1942)

Chicken corn soup. Dandelion salad. Doughnuts. Sauerkraut. *Schnitz* and *knepp*. *Schmier kase*. *Lattwerk*. Shoofly pie. Sand-tarts. These memorable foods from my childhood always take me back to the homes of my Amish grandmothers and aunts. To my mother's kitchen and the flavor-filled foods she prepares with such an easy, self-effacing flair.

She makes a fine chicken corn soup and every fall chops and ferments a dozen or so cabbages, filling her canning shelves with sauerkraut no grocery store variety I've ever used has matched. One of my sisters-in-law keeps an old tradition alive by creating the labor-intensive *schmier kase* from cheese curds, baking soda, and water. This unusual Pennsylvania German spread, which is cooked, cooled, and beaten at fifteen-minute intervals until light and foamy, flows over homemade rolls and actually melts in the mouth. Another of my sisters-in-law bakes a wet-bottom shoofly pie as good as any found in the bakeries of Lancaster County.

Dandelion salad and *schnitz* and *knepp* (ham with apples and dumplings) may adorn, on rare occasion, one or another of our tables, but most of us buy doughnuts and *lattwerk* (apple butter) because their production takes too much time. And my four sisters and I have done our utmost to reproduce the old family sand-tart recipe. Our fond memories of helping *Mummy* (Grandma) and Aunt Sarah bake these delightful Christmas treats have led us down many dead-end paths. We have not been able to turn out the thin, delicate wonders these two women made by the dozen. "Who might have that recipe?" we keep asking each other every year. The answer may well be "No one," for our grandmother and aunt were classic country cooks, producing their culinary wonders by feel and taste.

Written recipes seldom aid the re-creation of food prepared in this fashion because measurements are fluid, depending on the quality of the ingredients, the temperature of the kitchen, and even the whim of the creator. When I ask my mother for a recipe, she always recites it orally, peppering her recitation with phrases like "Cut up several stalks of celery, depending how large the stalk is" and "Add a ham hock, whatever size you want, I usually use a small one" and "Fill the kettle with milk." It's a tough act to follow.

Whatever our regional or family food tradition—African, Cajun, Mexican, Cuban, or any of the folkways that inform cooking in our time—we will probably find the only way to keep the memory alive is to cook. If we want to remember how to make gumbo and tortillas, hoppin' John and sweet-potato pone, or matzo-ball soup and liverwurst, we will have to cook. It's just that simple.

And just that incredibly difficult. Most of us have little time or energy for fussing with food. Our lives, consumed as they are with professional obligations and family demands, require us to cut corners and subsist on prepackaged foods and delicatessen or restaurant offerings. It's regrettable and expensive.

Maybe, though, we can find a few simple, small ways to retrieve and retain our food memories. Why not devote an occasional weekend to cooking like our mothers and grandmothers? Or an evening to making dinner from scratch, inviting our families to join in the fun? Or a Saturday afternoon to baking pies or cakes or even doughnuts?

Our mothers' recipes will survive if we use them. That's what the Amish women who raised me always thought. That's probably what many of our mothers and grandmothers think.

Justice Laced with Forgiveness

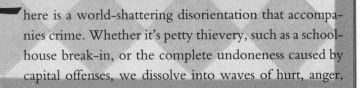

Justice is like the Kingdom of God—it is not without us as a fact, it is within us as a great yearning.
—GEORGE ELIOT,
Romola (1862)

There is a world-shattering disorientation that accompanies crime. Whether it's petty thievery, such as a schoolhouse break-in, or the complete undoneness caused by capital offenses, we dissolve into waves of hurt, anger, and hate. Few things are as terrifying as becoming the victim of a crime.

A distinct vulnerability to violence hangs over all of us. When we are wise, we learn never to take safety for granted. We reach for the relative security of familiarity, weaving unseen nets of protection around ourselves and our homes. We strengthen the nets with reasonable precautions, moving with purposeful gait and locking our cars and houses. We also take risks—walking the streets or opening doors to strangers—because to do otherwise is to surrender to paranoia and fear.

Like us, my people know there is risk in their manner of life. In driving slow-moving buggies on back country roads late at night. In resolving never to take up arms, not even in self-defense. In living by a code of peacefulness even in the proximity of violence. But most are resolute—fear must not rule their reality.

When several Amish buggies were held up late one Sunday night by thrill-seeking teenagers on a rural road, a newspaper reporter with a tinge of incredulity in his voice asked me, "What were those buggies doing out on the road after midnight?" The answer surprised him. Going home. Going home after an evening with friends. Going home. Such an ordinary activity for young people everywhere.

The more weighty questions, I thought, might have been directed to parents or friends of the thrill seekers. "Why did they have guns? What do you think possessed them to prey on other people?" No one was physically hurt in these incidents, and the buggy drivers immediately stopped at neighboring farms to call the police. The offenders were caught, registering surprise that the crimes had been reported.

Which brings us to the much larger questions of justice and forgiveness. My people generally trust local justice systems, and they actively seek compensation for vandalism and petty crime. They desire redress and quickly agree to prosecution when they become victims of violence, expressing the hopeless anger and terrible fear we all feel in the presence of such overwhelming wrong. They may even have the courage to face their offenders, hoping to retrieve stolen property or instill in the perpetrator some sense of the pain and suffering he or she has caused.

We live in a complex society in which none of the questions about crime and its pervasive presence are easy. Beyond a hope for justice, my people search for ways to go on with their lives and restore some sense of normality to their world. They stand beside each other, listening to the stories of loss and pain. They ask no one to blithely forgive, but they teach forgiveness—that life-changing force that will seldom heal the offender but always heal the victim.

Forgiveness

Surely it is much more generous to forgive and remember, than to forgive and forget.
—MARIA EDGEWORTH
(1787)

orgive those who wrong you. My people make no apologies for practicing this high art of human expression. They
consider forgiveness an essential element of community life.
"Have you forgiven?" is a common query among Amish
women when one has been seriously wronged. And when forgiveness
does not come easy or soon, paragraphs of advice include such sen-

tences as "You need to work on forgiving" or "You're only hurting yourself if you don't forgive." My people also realize that extending pardon is not always simple and that the process of working on forgiveness may require patience and time. Indeed, a forgiving life is both as difficult and as luminous an achievement as any transforming work of art.

The cathartic novels of Joyce Carol Oates. The wheat fields and haystacks of Van Gogh. The voice of Kathleen Battle. The preparation and serving of a fine dinner. The solid construction of a house by a careful carpenter. The thoughtful love and nurture of a child. All are works of art. All exact from the artist a profound combination of mind-numbing work and effortless grace.

It is the same with a forgiving life. The melodic notes, the brush-strokes, the penmanship of forgiveness lift us from the limitations of personal emotions and feelings. The work of forgiveness begins to free us from the ropes that bind us to the hurt. In the process, we may need to write hundreds of pages, discard countless canvases, and re-hearse the notes until we no longer miss them. For it takes both the failure and success of practice to make the finished product won-drously inspirational.

Like the artist, we will be most blessed when we let go. For only when the novel is published, the painting shown, and the song performed can they begin their work of transcendence. In forgiveness, as in art, the journey from the work in progress to the finished piece may be a slow one. But it is the letting go, the moving on, that frees us to begin working on the next novel, painting, or song. Which is no small feat for an artist.

Some writers expend a lifetime on one novel. Some painters never show their work. Some singers stop singing. The sadness of their stories is often shattering. It is the same when we cannot forgive.

And it is so very different when we let go. Whatever the hurts that shadow our lives, may we begin the long journey to letting them go. May we resurrect the buried pain and work through the troubles in ways most helpful to us. Maybe we see a therapist. Maybe we talk to a friend. Maybe we find a support system to undergird and stand beside us in the work of forgiving the person or persons who wronged us.

We begin to forgive when we realize, as my people have always said, that forgiveness helps us most of all. Like any great work of art, forgiveness first transforms the artist. Then it touches the audience, multiplying mercy and making the world a better place.

LOUISE STOLTZFUS

❦ ❦

A Simple Tool for Resolving Anger

*D*o not let the sun go down while you are still angry.

—*Book of the Ephesians*

*L*et not the sun go down upon your wrath. The King James version of this scripture in Ephesians is often quoted among Amish women. A simple tool of civility, it has kept many women from making mountains out of molehills. On one level, it is an ideal; a tool, not a law. On another level, it is something my people literally try to uphold. They work to resolve anger and hurt before going to bed at night.

I have floated this theory among different groups of women in the years since I left the Amish. It seldom stays above water very long and is often pushed down and drowned for its simplistic view of human nature. This is, of course, the point. Women who are Amish want to keep life simple. Keeping relationships simple helps to keep life simple.

My people generally do not wish to entangle themselves in the mysteries of psychological analysis. The complexities of the human mind confound all of us. Too much examination, my people believe, can turn the tiniest misunderstanding into growing layers of difference and distance.

It is true, the more we educate ourselves about human behavior, the harder we work at deciphering other people. Every action of a child, friend, or spouse has to have a reason. And every reaction generates extensive investigation. We are often caught in an out-of-control spin of detailed conversations and arguments with no end. The sun comes up, the sun goes down, we never skip a beat. Our lives are trivialized into recitations of "I can't believe you're doing that again."

This is not the way of Amish women. They rely on the simple tool of resolving small differences as soon as possible and hopefully before the sun goes down. Many are quite good at expressing their anger, at letting their children, husbands, or friends know they've been hurt. But rather than analyzing the reasons for the behavior or spinning out all its possible explanations, they prefer to say, "I'm going to let this go. I'm going to let my anger go." This objective frees them to talk with their spouses and friends about their children, the books they read, the problems of a parent, or the philosophies they espouse.

Some forms of pain and hurt are indeed mountains that compel us to action and anger, as well as years of discussion and working on forgiveness. This does not mean that every slight, every tiny misdeed, should be treated with equal weight. That is what my people mean when they talk about not letting the sun set on their wrath.

We may not choose the Amish way. We may legitimately find it too simplistic. But as we work at intimacy and relationships, let us find tools in our own heritage and life understandings that help us to easily resolve the anger and hurt of small differences, that keep the molehills from becoming mountains and give us many nights of peaceful rest.

Finding Freedom in Chaos

We are most deeply asleep at the switch when we
fancy we control any switches at all.
—ANNIE DILLARD,
Holy the Firm (1977)

Chaos or control? Avoiding the one by exercising the other
consumes much of the energy we expend every day of our
lives. For good reasons. If you don't have a plan for cleaning
your house, you'll have squalor. If you don't have a plan
for getting to work on time, you'll lose your job. If you don't have a

plan for raising your children, you might lose them. Sometimes, though, we allow this energy to turn into a much darker force—an obsession with controlling every aspect of our existence, including the people who depend on us.

Years ago I drove to school along a highway lined on both sides by Amish farms and homesteads. As I passed one such house, I couldn't help but notice the extreme care these folks took with the exterior appearance of their home. Every year they trimmed the three maple trees in their lawn into perfect round shapes. Every year! Those glorious trees that love nothing more than to be chaotic and a little crazy in the shapes and forms they take. Finally, one of the trees rebelled. About ten branches along one of its lower sides died. Just like that. No buds. No green leaves. Just ugly bare branches reaching for the sky.

I waited anxiously to see if the tree might muster the strength to come back. Then one morning it was gone. Cut down. Destroyed. Put away. Sacrificed to conquer a tiny bit of chaos and regain control of the environment. Whenever I feel the urge to enlist extraordinary means to control my life, I remember that maple and its masters.

I also remember another Amish woman and the matter-of-factness with which she speaks of the many calamities her family has endured.

The loss of a beloved aunt in a tragic neighborhood killing. A devastating house fire. Broken limbs and eye surgeries. None of which have diminished her faith or the deep conviction that a higher power controls the circumstances of her life and would never give her anything she could not bear.

Somewhere between these two Amish expressions we will find ourselves. Absolute control, no matter how desperately we reach for it, is a complete myth. An obsessive need to manage our surroundings changes nothing. Pain and trouble will come. So will pleasure and success. We can schedule and trim and clean, but we cannot prevent decay and death. If we insist on control, we will only increase our burdens and drive those around us into rebellion and despair.

Accepting chaos liberates both our minds and bodies and releases a fulfilling life force. A force that fills our lawns with sprawling maple trees. Our homes with happy children. Our places of work with pleasantness. We will not be able to avert problems, but we will be free. We will slowly come to know that we cannot isolate ourselves from trial and trouble. We can only work at accepting chaos as it appears.

Living with Imperfection

When we do the best that we can, we never know what miracle is wrought in our life, or in the life of another.

—HELEN KELLER,
Out of the Dark (1914)

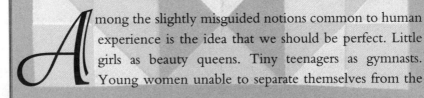

Among the slightly misguided notions common to human experience is the idea that we should be perfect. Little girls as beauty queens. Tiny teenagers as gymnasts. Young women unable to separate themselves from the fact that models are skinny and waiflike only because they don't eat and not because they have enviable lives.

Some members of the media exult in the wondrous perfection of a child's lovely, adultlike face and hairstyle. Or the expert balance-beam techniques of a very young woman. Or the flawless body of a model. Yet they often neglect to remind us that these so-called examples of perfection seldom house the bodies of children and young people with well-rounded, whole lives.

And that is where we have to start. By letting ourselves and each other off the hook of perfection. That's what I learned from the women who raised me. How many thousand times I must have heard them say, "Nobody's perfect."

Nobody is perfect. We all have limitations—physical, emotional, spiritual. How we compensate, what we do with the gifts and capabilities we have, matters a great deal more than either the perceived presence or absence of perfection.

Rachel tells me a story about how this works in Amish life. Her brother, who runs the family farm, injured his arm in a fall during the busiest weeks of spring. He couldn't plant corn and came close to despair over the unfortunate timing of his accident. Until he thought about asking his older brother, born with a serious mental handicap, to rise to the task. "Physically, Sam is in excellent shape, and he did a good job that year with the corn," Rachel says. This theme of integration is a common one among my people. Family members with disabilities are included in the general life. Schools for special children are often located in the same building as a regular school "so the children get to interact with others."

Living with imperfection challenges us to do the best we can. To accept that our bodies may never resemble those of pampered fashion models and movie stars. To rise to the heights of our own abilities, whatever they may be, but also to pardon ourselves for being human. To take joy in the miracles that happen when we let go of the impulse toward perfection.

Imperfections often make us more beautiful. This is true in much of life. The thorns on a rose stem. The clouds against a perfect blue sky. The knots in a grain of wood that give a piece of furniture its character. The thorns and knots in our bodies and minds that inspire us to strive for excellence.

Let us forget about perfection and reach instead for excellence. Excellence is about winning marathons and Olympic gold medals. It is also about placing tenth in a race while running a personal-best time. It is also about falling across the finish line far behind the winners.

A Quiver Full of Children

What a difference it makes to come home to a child!
—MARGARET FULLER,
letter (1849)

I do not have children. My decision not to marry the young man who wanted me when I was twenty-one changed my life forever. Had I married him, I would most likely have settled into a traditional, plain life with, as my people say, a quiver full of children. Not having married him was the right decision. Not having children is a decision about which I have remained much more ambivalent.

Among my people, the expectations are simple and uncomplicated. Those who do not marry do not have children. Those who marry have as many children as their combined fertility permits. While Amish couples occasionally seek advice from doctors about moderate forms of contraception such as the rhythm method, they do so very quietly. Those few (sometimes for health reasons) who use more radical controls—condoms, diaphragms, and, very rarely, pills—do so with great secrecy and without seeking the blessing of the church. Most follow in the steps of their parents and grandparents and have many children.

Amish women in general will not speak on the record about this deeply personal question. "These are private matters" is a firm declaration that rules much of what my people choose not to say about birth control. Among themselves they urge "keeping private things private" while also advising each other to live within the conventions of the church. Mothers may admonish their daughters not to use birth control. But if a church leader were to comment publicly about such an intimate matter, most people would question his lack of discretion and approach him for his poor judgment. Instead of preaching against the use of birth control, sermons often focus on the blessings of having children: "Children are a gift of God. You will be happy when you have as many as God chooses to give you."

This is, I think, an example of a particular strength in Amish cultural understandings. Opinion makers, both men and women, commonly spend more time speaking for an idea or principle rather than speaking against its opposite impulse. They extol the virtues of plain clothing rather than lamenting the fashions of the world. They support and maintain strong school systems while spending relatively little time attacking the public schools. They teach couples to desire children rather than demanding that they never use any form of birth control.

In speaking for children, for wanting and welcoming children, my people raise up parents prepared to nurture and care for the young. Parents who understand the consuming responsibilities of having a family. Parents who have a mutual support structure for giving children happy homes.

Whether or not we have children of our own, we would all do well to spend more time speaking for children, protecting their place in family life, and offering them our unconditional love. Which is where I find myself as I enter middle age. Not having children does not exempt me from having a responsibility to children. To speak for them. To welcome them. To love them without question. To be part of a larger community that helps to keep them well.

Reinventing Our World for Children

The character and history of each child may be a
new and poetic experience for the parent.
—MARGARET FULLER,
Summer on the Lakes (1844)

Several years ago there was an AT&T commercial that must
surely have pulled at the heartstrings of every working
mother. It depicted a household full of activity with a thirty-
something mother in sharp business attire. As she directed

her casually dressed children through the routine of the baby-sitter's arrival, one little girl requested a half-dozen favors, all of which got a soft and reasonably worded no. Finally, the mother said, "Honey, you know I need to go see a very important client?"

"Mommy, when can I be a client?" And Mommy melted.

"You have five minutes to get ready for the beach." Ten seconds later children romped in the sand while Mommy talked to her client by cell phone from a beach chair.

The commercial worked. And it illustrated in living color the tug-of-war between home and job that catches many of us in its grip. We are competent women with careers. We believe the coming of children should not change our lives any more than their coming should change the lives of the men who are their fathers.

We want to work. Or we don't want to work, but we need the money. Sometimes we are raising children alone. In any event, we must make a choice, a choice accompanied by an ocean of compromises no matter which of the divergent roads we go down. It is never easy.

The women in my family, even those who are not Amish, have always stayed home. My grandmothers. My mother. My sisters. My sisters-in-law. They have made sacrifices to subsidize their decisions.

Some rarely go out to eat. Some have not been able to purchase their own homes. Some have never taken an expensive summer vacation.

I cannot be sure what I would do if I had children. I think I would break with family tradition. Not because I do not respect and admire these women in my family. Not because I think they have inferior lives. Not because I disagree with them. In their unstinting commitments to home and family, their worlds have expanded to places I could never dream of going. I just think I would have a hard time giving up my career. Which is, of course, the dilemma for every mother, whatever her choices. "What am I missing? What will I regret?"

Amish women have seldom been ambivalent about this. A mother needs to be at home. But so does a father. I think my people are onto something. Many fathers are farmers, yes. But land is scarce in some Amish communities, and these families have responded by opening hundreds of small businesses—bookstores, greenhouses, woodworking shops. "That way the fathers can still be close by" is how Amish women often explain this transition from farms to small businesses, rather than from farms to factory jobs.

Many young mothers and fathers in our own society have also made similar decisions, setting up computer workstations in home offices. I think it signals significant changes in how business operates, and I hope we will be wise enough to adapt to the changes and to accommodate what my people will always applaud as the best way. Mother and father together reinventing their world to be with their children.

Creative Discipline

It takes hard work and hard thinking to rear good
people.
—MARGUERITE KELLY AND ELIA PARSONS,
The Mother's Almanac (1975)

I wondered whether consciousness-raising in the larger society
about problems such as the negative effects of spanking has
had any effect on the way discipline is taught and practiced
in Amish society. So I asked an Amish friend and former
schoolteacher about it. The first part of her answer I expected; it was

the second part that intrigued me. "Children need to be taught obedience, but you don't need to be cruel to get the lesson across. I always tried to be thoughtful and creative." I asked her what she meant by creative discipline.

Her eyes brightened as she told a collection of stories, including one about a seventh grader who was a daydreamer. "He just could not stay focused. I moved his desk to a place where he would have fewer distractions, but he sat for long stretches and stared into space. This went on for several years, as I tried to understand whether he had some medical problem." She prayed about it, agonized over a solution, and then one evening had a revelation.

The next morning she called the boy aside before ringing the school bell. "I've tried to understand why you can't get your lessons done on time. Maybe it's because you're too tired. So today I want you to rest all day. I don't want you to do any work at all. Just sit at your desk and rest." At recess he wanted to play, but she advised him that he was probably too tired. "You can sit on the porch and watch the other children. I'll come and sit with you. But you can't play because you're just too tired." Mid-afternoon, he wanted to at least write his assignments down. "Oh no," she said. "You don't have to do them. You're just too tired, and you need to rest." At the end of the day, she reminded him that as long as he continued to daydream, she would declare an occasional day of rest. He went home.

The next morning he came to her, "Teacher, I'm not tired! And I don't ever want a day of rest again." By noon he was back on track with his work and, inspired by the memories of his day of rest, seldom missed getting his lessons done on time during his last two years in school.

Did she ever spank anyone, I asked her. "Yes, a few times. But only as a last resort. We teachers used to remind each other that only if you hated to spank more than the child hated the spanking was it appropriate."

My people are caught in the same dilemma women and men everywhere encounter with discipline. We don't always take the time or have the energy to be creative. Having learned from our parents or religious traditions that spanking rescues a child from him or herself, some of us come to believe it is a disciplinary measure we cannot avoid.

We are not unlike my friend Amy. A busy working mother of two preschoolers, she described an agonizing ambiguity about spanking,

"You don't want your child to grow up without discipline. Sometimes spanking seems like the only way to teach them. But, you know, the few times we've spanked, it hasn't really made a difference."

As child psychologists and social workers continue to raise questions about the wisdom of using violence to teach a child nonviolence, parents of all persuasions search for more creative solutions.

A letter to an Amish family magazine recently asked for help with a two-year-old who was throwing temper trantums. The editors printed seventeen letters of response. Many women responded with disclaimers like "Make no mistake, I do believe in spanking" but went on to plead with the parents to consider a possible root cause for the child's problems. One young mother clearly stated, "It is apparent that spanking is not solving this child's problem. Some parents have many regrets later for all the spankings they gave a certain problem child."

Her sad sentiments are echoed in many homes throughout our society. Perhaps we will find that creative discipline works just as well as more traditional methods. How will we know unless we follow the examples of those who are courageous and careful enough to try?

Singleness, Schools, and the Amish Story

The time is come when women must do something more than the "domestic hearth."

—FLORENCE NIGHTINGALE,
Cassandra (1852–1859)

In the village of Amish life, single women play many important roles. As beloved aunts, they add a layer of acceptance and warmth to many a young person's heart. As daughters, they stay with older parents, making the Amish tradition of caring for their own a continuing reality. As sisters and friends, they relieve harried young mothers with words of encouragement and occasional childcare. As women with successful careers, they break the married-with-children stereotype so many of us hold of the Amish way.

Arie is such a woman. "I like my life. I don't think I would be any happier as a married woman. My nieces and nephews have given me the joy I would have had in children of my own." She lives alone in a beautiful house overlooking a valley of Amish farms and has about her the solid sense of reason of a woman at peace with herself and her life circumstances. She rarely complains about what she doesn't have but rather laughs and smiles and quips about what she does have. A lovely home. Lots of friends. A good life.

As a single woman, I have long been inspired by Arie's example. For being single, or even married without children, is not an easy niche in our marriage- and family-oriented societies. But it is a reality for many women, Amish and non-Amish alike. The pressures that we, as women of the world, feel to get married and have children also exist among my people. While there is sometimes a veiled suspicion toward those who choose otherwise, there is also an honest effort to embrace singleness, to be sensitive and generous toward those who do not have children.

In a narrative that roughly parallels the current American women's movement and our success in the job market, many single Amish women have become more and more visible in their communities as they have answered the call to become schoolteachers. It's hard work for little pay, but teaching school has given these often bright, articulate women a stage from which to influence Amish thought, to mold and shape young lives, and to impress the future thinkers and leaders of the church. Few teachers would consciously recognize it, but these women have punctured the glass ceiling of the Amish partriarchy.

The proliferation of one-room Amish schools in the decades since my people won the right to educate their own children introduced something new to the Amish way—expansion and growth. After having struggled for centuries as a small group on the margins of the world, the Amish community doubled its population in the fifteen-year time span between 1974 and 1989. Young people stopped leaving. And they did so largely because their education revolved around the thought patterns of the Amish way.

While a few men have chosen to become teachers, most Amish schools are presided over by single women. Although they are almost never willing to think in such congratulatory terms, these women are the progenitors of a new Amish reality. A growing and vital church community.

The multifaceted roles of Amish single women invite us to be more thoughtful about the ways we typecast singleness in our own societies. Fulfillment does not equal marriage and family. Happiness can be found alone or in companionship without children as easily as in companionship with children. Life goes on whether or not we join with another person in the pursuit of a lifelong relationship and the challenges of raising a family.

Nephews and nieces need aunts and uncles. Parents and siblings need the stability and completeness single people or those married without children bring to the whole story of any village.

Children and Chores

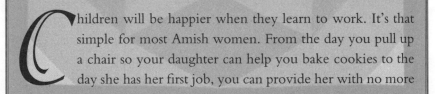

Young people, you don't know what hard work is until you have kept house and cooked as we did in those days at Cross Creek.

—IDELLA PARKER,
Idella (1992)

Children will be happier when they learn to work. It's that simple for most Amish women. From the day you pull up a chair so your daughter can help you bake cookies to the day she has her first job, you can provide her with no more important resource than to teach her to work. Yes, she may fuss and grumble. She may complain of your rigidity. She may recite a collection of grievances. But if you prevail, she will one day be thankful for your directions, for her knowledge of cooking and cleaning, and for the ethic of work that makes her life and home more satisfying. This is what my people believe about the predicaments of teaching children to work.

In the chaotic world of working families, teaching youngsters to help can sometimes seem more trouble than it's worth. They don't want to. We don't have the energy. We come home too tired to pry them from the TVs and computers. We do the work ourselves because we think it's less complicated that way.

Amish mothers have the same problems. Their children hide behind books and board games, and women among my people are also tempted to do the chores themselves. Until they stop to consider the consequences of not teaching their children to work.

These women begin with the premise that work is good. Mothers often join their children. Baking is fun when it includes sampling batter and dough, experimenting with colors and shapes, and eating the finished product fresh from the oven. Cleaning goes more quickly with the occasional promise "when this is done, we'll have lunch at the picnic table." While work changes from day to day, Amish mothers teach consistency by giving children ongoing responsibilities—feeding the dog, washing the dishes, hoeing the garden.

They believe that work also has direct benefits for the parent: She has less to do. An eight-year-old son who sweeps or vacuums the living room every evening gives his mother that much more time to sit and rest. A daughter who cleans the bathroom once a week makes it more possible for her mother to relax with a sewing project or good book. A fourteen-year-old who takes responsibility for mowing the lawn relieves his parents, yes, but he also eventually makes a better employee, causing less work and worry both for the people who raise him and those who hire him.

My people also believe that children who learn to work in an atmosphere of shared love live in happier homes. Mothers and fathers are less exhausted when they do not become servants. Sons and daughters take less for granted when they observe and participate in the direct connections between recreation, dirty clothes, and work. Families have more time to play together when everyone works together.

Those who are parents know. None of this is easy. There are no quick and easy solutions, no magic wands to wave. Just the persistent day-to-day words: "I need you to help me do this" and "Thank you for doing a good job." What my people do is remind each other of the benefits and the results. Happy homes. Pleasant children. More energetic parents. Young people better prepared for the world of work.

Read
to the Children

No entertainment is so cheap as reading, nor any
pleasure so lasting.
　　　　—Lady Mary Wortley Montagu,
　　　　　　letter (1753)

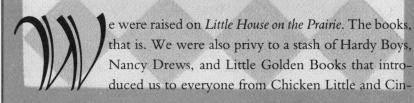

e were raised on *Little House on the Prairie*. The books,
that is. We were also privy to a stash of Hardy Boys,
Nancy Drews, and Little Golden Books that introduced us to everyone from Chicken Little and Cin-

derella to Snow White and Little Red Riding Hood. The spacious walk-through closet with books spilling from its shelves was in our beloved Aunt Sarah's room at *Mummy* and *Dawdy*'s house. A veritable treasure trove that changed as we grew older, it opened our eyes and minds to the wide world of knowledge and information.

The Little House series came into our home one book at a time. It was the 1960s. An age of turmoil and unrest. We grieved for John Kennedy and Martin Luther King Jr. We worried about the tumult of the time. In the evening, we escaped with Laura Ingalls and Almanzo Wilder to the romance of covered wagons and pioneer homesteads. We shivered through blizzards on the Plains and sweated out dust storms and hard times. When we finished the series, we started over.

One winter Mom and Dad decided to read the books aloud in installments that stretched for several years beyond that first season. We had no TV, but we had lots of books and vivid imaginations. Our parents loved to read, and they taught us to do the same. They read to us because they wanted to, because it gave them pleasure, and because we were entertained. In the way of most Amish parents, they also supervised our reading material, directing us toward stories and styles they considered appropriate. They were very wise. There would be plenty of time for broader discoveries later.

As my mom and dad did, many contemporary Amish parents also make a point of reading to their children. They subscribe to Amish-related periodicals such as *Family Life* and *Young Companion*. They buy lots of books, and they take their children to local libraries. "We try to visit the library about once a month," Mary tells me. She and her husband are book lovers, and they have educated themselves and their children through years of reading.

We might want to do the same. Reading is one of life's simplest, least expensive, and most accessible amusements. It entertains. It expands knowledge and transports us to people, places, and things we may never see or experience except through the window of a book. It has no equal for ordinary joy.

All of us need more moments of pure joy. We need the sense of stillness found behind the pages of a book. The luxury of moving nothing except our eyes and minds. And the fullness of connecting with the simple beauty and lyricism of words on paper.

Uncovering Racism with Intelligence

It is time for parents to teach young people early on that in diversity there is beauty and there is strength.
—MAYA ANGELOU,
Wouldn't Take Nothing for My Journey Now (1993)

People sometimes ask me, "Are the Amish racist?" When I posed the question to an Amish woman, she hesitated and very slowly replied, "I don't know . . . I would . . . I would have to say . . . we are much like the average American. Unfortunately . . . we all generalize about other people." I know how difficult it was for her, a deeply tolerant woman, to acknowledge the presence of ignorance among her people.

Deep-seated prejudices undo all of us. For each of us, there remains the personal challenge of uncovering and overcoming our own preconceived and wrong ideas about other races, cultures, and ethnic groups. This is hard work, but only as we embrace diversity will we begin to know the richness that comes from blending our various stories.

My people live in a relatively narrow world that sometimes limits their individual understanding of others. But as a group they tirelessly teach consideration and respect for other people. As victims of religious persecution during the Reformation, they have their own memory of intolerance. *The Martyrs' Mirror*, a voluminous history of those who died for the faith, occupies a place of honor, next to the Bible, in most Amish homes. Its images of oppression leave an indelible impression of the injustice bred when the abuse of power joins forces with intolerance.

I read parts of this book as a child. So do many other young Amish. Its lessons pass from generation to generation because, in the Amish view, the world has never been nor will it ever be a safe place. Four hundred years after their martyr experiences, my people remain wary of the dominant culture. Few take the absence of persecution for granted. In that sense, they are like many other minority groups. They are vulnerable.

Those with more recent histories and current stories of suffering know much more about the pain this sense of vulnerability engenders. Margaret Walker once wrote, "Racism is so extreme and so pervasive in our American society that no black individual lives in an atmosphere of freedom." While an Amish woman cannot feel the depth of this pain, she can identify with its causes. She recognizes the symptoms and the results; the unconscionable actions and behaviors of those who think themselves better, those who refuse to learn from others.

One of the requirements of an intelligent life, it seems to me, is hearing other stories. Hatred festers everywhere. We can dilute its power by listening to other people. No matter where we live—in suburban white enclaves, in the city, in suburban black enclaves, in rural villages, or on isolated Amish farms—acceptance grows exponentially when we are willing to know people who are different from us.

Walking side by side with those whose views of the world do not mirror our own changes every prejudice, unlocking the vast reserves of intelligence and tolerance present in our hearts and minds. We improve ourselves, the small world around us, and the larger world by extension as we open the doors to such communion and friendship.

Morality or Ethics?

The real nature of an ethic is that it does not become an ethic unless and until it goes into action.

—MARGARET HALSEY,
The Folks at Home (1952)

My people understand morality to be about the "thou shalt nots" of life. Do not drink. Do not smoke. Do not steal. Do not kill. Do not be promiscuous. They understand ethics, or what they often call right living, to be about the "thou shalts" of life. Be kind to others. Be respectful to your parents. Be wise in business. Be thoughtful in faith.

The Amish pay a great deal of attention to right living. They pay less attention to some of the moral standards championed by other Christian communities. They rarely pound the pulpits about the evils of drinking and smoking. They demonstrate marked suspicion of those who lay claim to clean, moral living. And they try to achieve a balance between expectations of perfection and the realities of life.

Barbara says, "I don't understand how a businessperson who doesn't pay what is owed can be a good Christian because of a clean, moral life." Frenie describes it this way: "I am more concerned about treating others with kindness and respect than I am about questioning those who might enjoy a cigar or a shot of brandy." And Leah: "I know many people don't understand why we grow tobacco, but to me it's more important to live right than to take a stand against something like tobacco. My mom talks about how the older ones used to smoke, even the women sometimes. They rolled their own cigars. You know those hand-rolled cigars weren't nearly as harmful as cigarettes with all that extra nicotine. Of course, we don't do that anymore."

This tension, though few Amish women would consciously recognize it as such, is indeed about the differences between morality and ethics. The issues, however, fuel much invigorating debate among my people. Some champion the traditional notions of morality, and they register embarrassment over those who plead the causes of right living as more important than flawless morals.

All agree, though, that right living must concern everyone. That the proactive behavior of living well requires doing, not just refusing to do. That the actions of right living manifest themselves in the way we treat other people. And that deficiencies in right living can never be covered up by a profession of high moral standards.

As more and more Amish families move from the farm into the world of small business, my people find their ethical standards put to increasingly tough challenges. Church and community leaders have been asking each other many hard questions about business ethics. What do you do when you miss a promised deadline with a shipment of wood products? What do you do when profits plummet and bills stack up? What do you do when a client refuses to pay?

Again, they recommend action. Talk to the wood products customer. Talk to creditors. When someone cannot pay you, exercise mercy but also expect them to pay. Don't just let them off the hook.

Take the story of an Amish businessperson with a client who

refused to pay. Instead of threatening collection agencies or lawsuits, the Amish man kindly and persistently asked for his money. One day, he dropped by the creditor's place of business and gave him a loaf of homemade bread. "It was a symbol of love, but I still want my money. I won't do business with him again until he pays me."

This businessperson's unusual behavior can only be described as the Amish way. It's also a vivid example of ethics in action, and it encourages all of us to reconsider our standard reactions to those who cause us concern and harm. For us it may not be as simple as baking bread, but it is as easy as exercising kindness and consistency. It is as easy as showing love and mercy without letting people off the hook.

Transcending the Mundane

$\mathcal{W}$ork is creativity accompanied by the comforting
realization that one is bringing forth something really
good and necessary.

—JENNY HEYNRICHS,
"Was Ist Arbeit?" (1866)

$\mathcal{T}$o many Amish women, the everyday chores we often
call boring and ordinary are as important, though they may
not be as interesting, to the natural order of life in the world
as is the impassioned search for creativity and personal ful-

fillment. The mundane tasks of being a homemaker—making beds, cleaning bathrooms, and dusting furniture—bring a seamless steadiness to their surroundings that moderates the high passion of imagination and invention.

When I asked Barbara to describe a typical day, she laughed heartily and said, "Well, you'll soon find out that I don't live a very exciting life." By an unexciting life, she meant that her days sort of flow together in an unbroken stream of preparing meals, washing dishes, doing laundry, and cleaning the kitchen. Each day, she said, also has its times of rest: meditation and prayer in the morning, perhaps a quick afternoon nap or a quiet early evening of reading the paper or talking to her grandchildren.

Barbara accurately surmised that my days as a working woman bear little resemblance to what she called "just my ordinary life." What she didn't expect was how much I admired her. How much I envied her for having found a balance between the extraordinary and the mundane.

She also took me into her parlor, where she keeps a quilt in frame and where she spends many hours stitching fabric and producing carefully wrought pieces of art. Her hobby, which is how she speaks of quilting, belies all her words about having an uninteresting personal story.

Indeed, what I often find most intriguing about women among my people is their gentle acceptance of the commonplace, which is almost always coupled with a flair for the extraordinary. Some are astonishingly good cooks. Some are writers. Some are artists. Some are networkers or accomplished caregivers. They exercise their gifts as they have time and opportunity, but they rarely put creative work ahead of the mundane tasks of every day. Instead, they appreciate the sanity and singlemindedness that these chores lend their lives. It is this that makes them most unlike many of us.

We dread the mundane. We envy adventure, not domesticity. "You're so domestic" is definitely not a compliment to most fast-track women. We laugh apologetically on Monday mornings when the answer to "How was your weekend?" is "I cleaned the refrigerator" or "We planted flowers" and turn quickly to hear a co-worker describe a thrilling movie or a hotel getaway. Why?

Why not celebrate domesticity? For it is indeed interwoven into the whole cloth of sane living. A home where people share in the regular work of the mundane will no doubt be cleaner and more comfortable. A home where we honor the commonplace as well as the extraordinary will bless us with levels of communion we cannot feel or experience in a similar celebration of escapism, of getting away from it all. My people are sure of this.

They prefer an evening of washing windows and planting gardens to an evening at the theater or a pricy restaurant. Sharing these simple tasks with their partners and families transcends the outward appearance of the ordinary. In their opinions, such sharing enriches their life together immeasurably.

We may not want to become domestic. But we can perhaps meet my people halfway, continuing to enjoy the extraordinary while also accepting and basking in the simple pleasures of the mundane. Maybe we will even begin to tell our Monday morning stories of domesticity with a zest that reveals the translucent joy of clean, attractive homes and everyday partnerships.

The Recovery
of Neighborhood

*T*he method of moral hygiene as of physical hygiene
is social cooperation. We do not walk into the Kingdom of Heaven one by one.
—M. P. FOLLETT,
The New State (1918)

*I*t doesn't matter where you visit the Amish. Indiana. Ontario. Holmes County, Ohio. Lancaster County, Pennsylvania. Or Sarasota, Florida. You will instantly notice a heightened sense of neighborhood. My people are rural, small-town folk with one notable exception—a vibrant settlement within the city of Sarasota.

The area of Sarasota where most of the sun coast Amish live is called Pinecraft, and it lies near the geographic center of this growing Gulf Coast city, only a few miles southeast of downtown. The citified Amish women and men who live in Sarasota get around with bicycles or public transportation because no horses are kept within the city proper. Their neighborhood has several churches, a few restaurants, a grocery store, and a post office.

As is true of many Amish communities, you can easily speed by on the nearby main highways and remain oblivious of the Amish presence. But in Sarasota, if you turn even one car length off the busy thoroughfares around Pinecraft, you are suddenly transported to a place where people walk from house to house, traffic slows to a crawl, and neighbors play shuffleboard or pitch quoits on backyard porches.

LOUISE STOLTZFUS

❧ ❧

My people have created a restful neighborhood in the middle of this ultramodern resort city.

Strong neighborhoods are important to many Amish women, and they work at being good neighbors to each other and the folks around them who are not Amish. By contrast, a sense of neighborhood eludes many Americans. It's hard work, especially when our geographical environs are so much more diverse than most Amish areas.

The inner-city block where I live is about one-half Latino, one-fourth African, and one-fourth European. We come from a broad range of historically different places, and the expressions of our daily lives range from Spanish to Pennsylvania Dutch to a wide range of English accents. Neighborhood for us is a daunting task, a constant challenge, but the civilizing grace of our community is the fact that we keep trying. We smile and wave and talk to one another. We plant flowers and paint porches. We make mistakes. We agonize over lost opportunities and rejoice over small successes.

Much of the hard work of being a good neighbor, I think, comes as a result of the disjunction between who we were and who we are. Most of us, unlike women among my people, come from a place not immediately recognizable. The people on my block, for example, have no way of knowing that I was once Amish. I have no context for understanding the village in Puerto Rico or Mexico that shaped their lives. I have only a limited knowledge of the Bermudan heritage of my next-door neighbor. Fostering an interest in each other's lives increases this fund of knowledge and decreases the disparities between our past and present lives. It also helps us to recover neighborhood.

Whether we live in a condominium complex, on a suburban street, or a city block, we will want to work at knowing our neighbors. This does not necessarily mean we become best friends, but it does mean we are respectful of each other and we work at overcoming the cultural differences that separate us. Sometimes, it's as easy as smiling and waving. Other times, it takes concentrated effort to step aside and have a conversation across a backyard fence. The increased level of security that comes from knowing our neighbors makes these small niceties worthwhile.

LOUISE STOLTZFUS

❀ ❀

The Simple American Dream

When strawberries go begging, and the sleek
Blue plums lie open to the blackbird's beak
We shall live well—we shall live very well.
—ELINOR WYLIE,
"Wild Peaches" (1921)

Many Amish women have an inborn and natural affinity for the simple life. They prefer gardening and preserving over packaged foods and weekly trips to the grocery store. They like not having to worry about the changing fashions and styles of each season. They enjoy the soft light of kerosene lanterns, seldom missing the convenience or expense of electricity.

This is a consciousness very different from the American dream mind-set in which two-parent families work long hours to afford opulent homes, dance lessons for the children, and holidays in the south of France. Or when we're not quite as rich, perhaps it's tract houses on suburban cul-de-sacs, T-ball for the boys, gym classes for the girls, and two-week summer vacations to the Grand Canyon or the Great Smokies.

Furthermore, Amish women rarely tell "Sally made good" stories— the stories that always seem to begin with some version of "Her mother was a homemaker and her father was an elementary-school teacher in a small, forgotten town." And continue with "Today Sally owns a multi-million-dollar corporation. She found the American dream."

My people ask why the American dream cannot as well be found

LOUISE STOLTZFUS

❀ ❀

281

in simplicity. Not spareness, but simplicity. Not in the absence of extravagance, but in its presence tempered with knowing when to stop, when the time has come to leave the remaining strawberries for the blackbird's beak.

Simplicity may appear as incongruent with extravagance as it would be to serve shoofly pie with caviar and Cornish game hens. It is true, Amish women, who make lots of shoofly pie, hardly ever prepare Cornish hens, and most would consider caviar wildly overrated.

But they are connoisseurs of good food, and they know how to set a fine table. Other than the magnificent pies and desserts, their good old-country cuisine includes distinctive turkey roasts, mashed potatoes and gravy, creamed celery, and deep-fried oysters—simple food that is also extravagantly sumptuous and filling.

My people appreciate and take pleasure in good food, well-kept homes, opportunities for their children, and occasional vacations. They are different because they wish to remember a lesson we sometimes miss. The lesson of knowing when to stop and rest, when to say, "We have enough. We do not need more wealth or more fun or more gadgets. We can be happy with each other in this house where we now live. With our children, our neighbors, and our friends." A different, perhaps, but much easier way of achieving the American dream.

The Fleeting Nature of Fame

Fame is a fickle food
upon a shifting plate.
—EMILY DICKINSON,
"The Single Hound" (pub. 1914)

In the modern psyche, there lies a powerful attraction to fame and the imagined charms of celebrity. The fact that Andy Warhol's "Everyone gets their fifteen minutes of fame" exists demonstrates how completely many of us are sucked into this cycle. It's the reason we are willing to appear on daytime talk shows. It's the reason the gossip sheets and tabloids thrive. It's the reason we tune in whenever the evening news promises a tidbit or tiny twist in the life of a famous person.

When one of my Amish friends wrote a book, I asked her what would happen if she became famous. The shock in her eyes let me know that she had not even considered the possibility. Though she had been willing to write her family story, she definitely did not want the telling to disrupt her quiet country home, her calm Amish world, or her life as a humble farm woman. She had no desire for the limelight, no energy for the bright rays of fame. And she would make sure her slow dance with simplicity was not interrupted by the unsatisfying lure of a brief run with celebrity.

To strive for fame goes against the very nature of the Amish way. My people are much more interested in the firm ground of long-term friendships, the stable infrastructure of a well-tended community. To them watching out for everyone and conducting themselves with humility and grace always take precedence over a proverbial fifteen-minute fling with personal fame.

The belief that "we should not put ourselves forward" so permeates the entire body of their culture that those who yield to the temptations of fame receive constant reminders of the fleeting nature of being well known. It is not the stuff of real life, they say. Many times my people have responded with admonitions and kind warnings when I've admitted my own enchantment with celebrity.

Do not put yourself forward. In the trenches of daily experience, this is a difficult lesson for some of us to learn. We want people to notice. We want to be recognized. But these desires can trap us in an all-consuming need to thrust ourselves into the spotlight at every opportunity. Most Amish women understand the importance of not succumbing to such narcissistic impulses.

My people believe we will have happier and less complex lives when we do not yield to the charms of popular acclaim. For the whirl of such a life can never replace the security of a strong community and the blessings of quietness and serenity. Whatever the level of our own celebrity, may we find ways to embark on a search for humility, leaving far behind the soon forgotten vanity of fifteen minutes before the fickle camera of fame.

LOUISE STOLTZFUS

Her Hair, the Glory of Her Head

But if a woman have long hair, it is a glory to her.
—First Book of the Corinthians

It can be a burden, but it's also a source of supreme beauty and comfort. In *Braided Lives*, Marge Piercy writes, "I keep [my hair] long because I love the way it feels, part cloak, part fan, part mane, part security blanket."

While bad-hair days sometimes cloud our perceptions, most of us like our hair, whether long or short. We love running our fingers through it. We love the sensation of other fingers running through it. We experiment and play with styles, trying different brush strokes or advising the hairdresser to give us a new look. We worry and fret. We color and comb. We fuss over long golden manes, jet-black curls, or short distinguished gray.

Even when I was still Amish, I loved when others noticed and commented about "your beautiful hair." In those days, mine was long and black. I had never cut it and when I let it down, I could sit on its flowing ends. Still, like most other Amish women, I humbly complied with the ways of my people and seldom ever wore it long and loose.

The way Amish women wear their hair has intensely spiritual connotations for my people. It is the glory of the head. It should never be cut, but it must also never be flaunted. Rolling it into an elaborate configuration, an Amish woman pins her hair tightly against her head and covers it with a white, see-through, organdy head covering. The covering symbolizes her willingness to live an unselfish and modest life in full submission to her community. Only in private—when she is alone with friends or with her husband—does she reveal the glory, removing the covering and allowing her hair to fall across her shoulders and body.

LOUISE STOLTZFUS

❀ ❀

Those of us enamored with the celebration of individual beauty can scarcely comprehend such a mind-set. Why would any woman want to hide her loveliness? Why would she agree to cover her hair? It is impossible to address these questions in the context of individualism. We can only understand when we step outside ourselves, however briefly, and enter the Amish world, where the preservation of community matters more than individual freedom or beauty.

The scripture about a woman's hair being the glory of her head is cited so often among my people that it becomes an unforgettable part of most Amish women's consciousness. It's still one of the first things I think of when I think of my hair. Expectations are clear, and Amish women do their best to wear their hair as the community desires. But they also learn to love their hair, gladly hearing the words, "But if a woman have long hair, it is a glory to her."

When we feel the frustrations with so-called bad hair, we might stop and give thanks for its beauty. Through all our days, it will add a unique signature to our bodies. Whatever we as women do with this "glory of our head," we can be forever grateful for the elegance and poise it adds, whether the flowing manes and gentle curls of youth or the smooth layers and cropped gray of old age.

Amish Exercise and the Simple Life

What delights us in visible beauty is the invisible.
—MARIE VON EBNER-ESCHENBACH,
Aphorisms (1893)

If we suspect Amish women don't need to exercise because they work so hard, we're right. At least, we're right about most Amish women. Because women among my people have their own opinions and preferences, some occasionally supplement the discipline of labor with routine physical workouts such as long walks along country lanes. Especially as they grow older. Older women and single women often have fewer responsibilities and more time for recreational exercise.

Most, however, get their exercise from the hard work of living on a farm and raising a family. Their feet and legs pump treadle machines as they sew the family clothing. They dash up and down steps, from barn to house, running hither and yon after youngsters while completing the chores that fill a busy mother's day. They mow the lawn, hoe the garden, and help with the farmwork. They milk cows and make hay. They laugh together over an old saying, "A man works from sun to sun, a woman's work is never done," and keep right on going. There are few couch potatoes among Amish women.

They like to look and feel good, but they do not obsess about having perfect bodies. My people have a unique set of cultural understandings about perfection and living well. They are largely free and separated from the influences of popular culture. No TVs. No *Cosmopolitan* or *Seventeen*. No peer pressure created by the idolizing of movie stars and celebrities.

They have a much broader sense of beauty. In their eyes, a woman can never use makeup in her life and yet be very beautiful. She can be fifty pounds overweight and be beautiful. She can have crooked teeth and an imperfectly shaped hip or leg and still be beautiful. For beauty comes from within. It is an expression of the inner life that no amount of outer perfection or imperfection can ever change.

It's an arresting notion for the perfection-obsessed modern ego. How much simpler our lives would be if we didn't feel pressured to spend precious minutes of every morning applying makeup. How much simpler our lives would be if we didn't feel guilty about a few extra pounds, rushing out to buy the latest diet drink or join in the latest exercise craze. How much simpler our lives would be if we trusted each other to look beyond the imperfect outer self to the beauty within.

We can do it. The next time we're tempted to sink a few thousand hard-earned dollars into an aerobics class or a Nautilus machine, we might consider the Amish way. We might ask whether the same benefits could come to us free with regular walks in the park, a few hours in a garden, or a ball game with our children. We might be surprised. And we might emerge with more pleasant, less complicated lives.

Work Hard and Rest Well

Come to me, all you who are weary and burdened,
and I will give you rest.
—JESUS,
Book of Matthew

To be able to work hard and rest well. That is an Amish woman's opinion of great peace and bliss. My people are essentially blue-collar workers, women and men who enjoy the intensity of working until every bone and muscle in the body aches. Until they are, as they say, "tired out."

When they come in from such a quest, they long for a bed and a night of unbroken sleep, for they love with equal passion the ecstasy of complete rest.

Most of us understand working hard. We come home with the tired arms and legs of teachers, nurses, and waitresses or the exhausted eyes and minds of computer programmers and secretaries. We are very good at working hard. Unfortunately, we are not nearly as good at resting well.

A short, midday siesta revives many an Amish woman for an afternoon of throwing hay bales or planting a garden. An early bedtime energizes her to rise with the sun for a round of milking cows or getting children off to school. My people revel in the freedom that being homemakers gives them to manage the busyness of their days. They often ask each other, "Are you finding time to rest?"

This is a question my mother has asked me many times with great concern. When it seems especially impossible for me to step aside from deadlines and promises, I admit to her that in the immediate moment the answer is probably no. She prays for me. And she encourages me to make the time.

Time to rest. Time to sit in quiet places with eyes closed and mind still. Time to lie in bed, releasing the tension of hard work from the sinews and tendons of the body. Time to liberate the brain from its constant stimuli, letting our emotions slowly unwind.

Rest is, after all, an integral part of a resourceful life. A mind so tired it cannot think will not produce creative labor. A body so tired it cannot go on will not bring the hay into the barn. Rest restores the body and mind and rejuvenates the spirit and soul.

Though we have realities that may prevent us from taking midday siestas, we will be more peaceful as we learn to structure resting well into the hard work of our days and nights. Maybe we recline in our hammocks at six in the evening, scheduling family dinners around a time of rest. Maybe we trade five days of working hard for long, relaxing weekends. Maybe we plan ahead and schedule vacations to follow trying seasons of work.

Throughout her life, my mother has demonstrated an exquisite balance between working hard and resting well. I know how healthy and wise she is whenever I push the outer edges of rational behavior because of my obsession with work. I will always wish to be more like her. May we all have mothers or others who inspire us to follow the simple wisdom of rest after work.

Going to Church

*O*ne can be coerced to church, but not to worship.
—GEORGIA HARKNESS,
The Resources of Religion (1936)

*I*t's a novel idea. Having church services only every other Sunday instead of every Sunday. It's also a long-standing tradition among my people. Horses and buggies make getting to worship services a bigger undertaking than it is for those of us with cars and quick drives to nearby chapels or synagogues. Rooted in the practical consideration of convenience, church every other

Sunday has become a treasured Amish custom. "We like it like this" is the common refrain of many Amish women.

My people also think of the Sunday morning service as more than an hour-long singing, praying, and preaching event. Church, the Amish way, is an all-day affair where members of geographically arranged districts take turns to host the neighborhood (150 to 200 people) in their homes. Few Amish worship in church buildings.

These community-gathering experiences feature four-hour worship services, meals at noon, afternoon visiting, and supper for those friends and family members who have traveled from a distance. The service itself is low key and low pressure. Parishioners listen quietly to long recitations from the Bible and written German prayers. They participate in exotic Gregorian-style chants of ancient German hymns. Little about an Amish worship service can be compared to the more typical Protestant church service with its revival hymns and anxiety-ridden sermons.

"I guess you could say we like things to be slower and more reverent. We like to have a good order in our church" is how Malinda describes the Amish way of worship.

Preparing a home for these services takes hours of work for the women of the household. Which is, without doubt, another reason most Amish women have no interest in going to church every Sunday. Furniture must be stored to make room for church benches. Floors must be cleaned. Food must be prepared. Few women have a desire to go through this ritual twice as often.

In my childhood home, we children always looked forward to the Sunday off. It was a chance to sleep in and enjoy a leisurely, late-morning breakfast, a time to be together with our parents. I think this built-in permission to be flexible about attending worship services ultimately saved me from disliking church and is, perhaps, the primary reason I still go.

Leaving the Amish changed everything for me. My search for a religious home has led me through many congregations, most of whom have had very different expectations from the Amish. In these various persuasions, I have been expected to go to church every Sunday. And to Sunday school. And sometimes even to Wednesday evening prayer meetings. I have often felt oppressed by this extraordinary emphasis on worship, and I have seldom wished to fully engage in the high expectations of these groups, which always leaves me thankful for the more elastic structures of my childhood. Thankful for the wisdom of a tradition that supports balance around the questions of God and worship. Thankful for the symmetry between family and church. Thankful for the blessing of long worship services and the freedom not to go every Sunday.

The questions of church, faith, and worship are not easy to resolve. Whatever our traditions and stories, may we find religious homes that fit our personal hopes and dreams. Places where we and our children are nurtured. Places from which neither we nor our children feel the need to run.

The Oil
of Kindness

*T*rue politeness is to social life what oil is to machinery, a thing to oil the ruts and grooves of existence.

—FRANCES ELLEN WATKINS HARPER,
"True and False Politeness" (1898)

*S*mall pleasantries. The courtesies of "pardon," "please," and "thank you." Of smiling. Of looking the person who holds the door for you in the eye and saying thank you, even when you could easily hold it yourself. Many Amish women do their best to practice and teach these simple skills for improving relationships.

Sometimes we women of the world overlook the healing power of these everyday gestures. We turn instead to complicated ideas and philosophies to solve our problems. We read books on recovery and self-help. We call on therapists to make us feel better and on pastors to lift our burdens.

In the workplace, we avoid politeness because we fear acquiring labels such as "too nice" or, heaven forbid, "passive-aggressive." Amish women do not think in these ways. They urge us instead to uphold and practice kindness in the places where we live and work.

Let's rise up. Let's not permit ourselves to be dragged into a culture of discourtesy. Impoliteness is no sign of strength. It shouts of weakness, a pervasive, energy-draining weakness. A weakness that breeds unhappiness in families and friendships. "You never even say thank you" becomes a major theme that can easily be changed with the recovery and revival of simple courtesies.

It is also a weakness that costs the American workplace untold sums in lost incentive and productivity. All of which can be maintained or regained when managers and executives exercise more of the simple grace of human kindness. When they say "please" and "thank you." And when they say the words sincerely and with thought.

My friend Rachel likes to say, "Tact is the oil of life." She knows that sincere kindness will go further in making her feel better, in making her co-workers, friends, and family members feel better, than all the carefully wrought philosophies and treatises about human behavior.

Kindness is free. You don't need to give a dozen roses. But you will need to say, "Honey, that was a great dinner. Thank you."

Thoughtfulness is easy. You don't need to give an employee who has finished a task and done a fine job a bonus. But you will need to say, "Thank you, this company needs and appreciates your work."

Generosity is simple. The roses and bonuses are also sometimes appropriate and important. They signal our commitment to the oil that keeps family life fluid and the workplace livable.

My people generally believe that the simplest solution to a problem is often the best one. Whether we are plain Amish women planting gardens and caring for children. Or waiters in busy restaurants. Or librarians dispensing information and books. Or lawyers racing from deposition to court to home. Whoever we are, we can and will multiply our own pleasure simply by being sincerely kind and polite.

Aunt Sarah's Afghan

We are rich only through what we give.
—ANNE-SOPHIE SWETCHINE,
The Writings of Madame Swetchine (1869)

As women of industrialized and ready-made societies, many of us know little about the union of fabric and thread. Amish women, on the other hand, frequently have strong feelings about crocheting, knitting, quilting, and sewing. They make their own clothing, but my people also enjoy these domestic arts because of the passion they have for fabric-related gifts—quilts, afghans, comforters, dolls, crocheted doilies, or knitted sweaters, socks, and caps.

Designed for caring and warmth, these gifts usually carry the maker's hope that she will not be forgotten. Though sometimes worn thin, many reappear years later in cedar chests and closets, holding the remnants of their stories. "Mother gave me this quilt when we got married" or "I played with that doll when I was a little girl" or "Oh, look, there are the booties Aunt Sarah knitted when you were a baby."

For many women, few things are quite as wonderful as rediscovering a piece of fiber art. We feel an intimate connection to the creator. As we smooth the wrinkled layers of an old quilt, comforter, or afghan, we remember a woman from our past whose hands toiled through the making of what she probably considered a practical gift. Perhaps the colors and designs surprise us. The sensations of the fabric transport us to another place and time. Or the frayed edges make us sad.

My aunt Sarah was such a woman. She especially loved knitting and filled her evenings with baskets of yarn flying through her fingers. "You just tell me what colors you want and I'll make you an afghan." It was a promise she kept, selecting three shades of blue for the "My favorite color is blue" period of my young life. It was a soft cover that comforted me through a voluntary-service assignment in Arkansas, a school-teaching job in Iowa, and the university in Florida. It still takes the chill off many late fall and early spring evenings, sometimes keeping my friends warm and always helping me to remember Aunt Sarah.

Such are the charms of a gift of fiber art. When New York's Whitney Museum of American Art hosted a sixty-one-piece quilt exhibition in 1971, the display reawakened a multitude of memories. The ensuing years have witnessed what some call "a quilt and sewing craze." Women everywhere pulled out their sewing machines and began to piece fabric.

An astonishing Amish Bars quilt in the collection prompted an avalanche of visitors to descend upon Amish communities, seeking what we now call antique Amish quilts. Women among my people suddenly found themselves with a lucrative source of income—making quilts and other fiber arts and crafts.

The world has subsequently come to their communities, flocking to village stores and farm homes to buy these wondrously simple gifts. Gifts that become part of family lore. "We bought that quilt from an Amish woman in Lancaster County" or "I gave you that doll when you were three years old" or "Oh, look, that's the handmade, knitted afghan Mom and Dad found in that tiny store in Amish country."

Whether we make stitched gifts or buy them from someone else, they have an allure reserved for the permanence of handmade items. A piece of furniture, a quilt, an afghan. There is something very different about these gifts. They transfer comfort, protection, and warmth. They have a story, and they help us to remember.

Peace Begins
at Home

*N*o institution can be good which does not tend to
improve the individual.

—MARGARET FULLER,
Memoirs (1840)

*I*t is an elusive reality. Peace. We wish for it within the four walls of our homes, in our local communities, and in the world. We worry about the brokenness of world affairs, the random acts of violence in our streets, the ethnic disintegration of civilized societies. We wonder, "Could it happen to us?"

The answer is yes. It could happen to us because disintegration and violence come from something, somewhere. The roots of these terrors are all too often at the disturbing center of a badly broken structure for bringing up children. World peace begins at home—one friendship, one thoughtful word at a time.

Home. That great harbinger of all that is good in the world. The one place where everyone deserves to be at peace. My people preach and practice something they call "the sanctity of home life."

To Amish women, the home is a sanctuary. When the home is successful, when it provides satisfaction and safe shelter to all who live there, it is more sacred than a church building. More to be desired than any other place in the world. More pleasant than a quiet spot in a park or a perfect summer evening on a beach.

This ideal can only be realized—in Amish society as in our own—when we begin by being deliberate about who will share our homes.

The sanctity of home and the seriousness of marriage are the two precepts my people uphold to illuminate and guide this pivotal life decision. My paternal grandmother and my mother, two women with wonderful marriages and happy homes, reminded me many times, "It is better to be single than to wish you had never married." I did, in fact, choose to be single, establishing a home that has become my rest and my refuge.

Those of us who enter into partnerships or begin raising families take a different set of risks. Peaceful living comes to depend on the give-and-take of our lives together. We can still make our homes places of peace, havens to which we return with full and grateful hearts. Places where children learn the lessons of living well with others. Places where we preserve wholeness by willingly receiving each new message of living well with our partners.

When we make a restful home our life's main priority, we have taken the first step in creating a peaceful society. Women and men who live in peace at home are able to transfer their skills to neighborhoods, to the workplace, to the larger society, and ultimately to the world.

Those who speak with voices of reason, who know how to show restraint, who can support the ideas of other people, are usually women and men whose lives are firmly grounded in the pursuit of living well at home. They share, more by assimilation than any other process, the gifts of civility with their neighbors, co-workers, and fellow citizens.

Let us do whatever we can (leave a bad situation if we must) to establish such homes for ourselves and our children. The world will one day thank us.

The Search for Home

Call it a clan, call it a network, call it a tribe, call it a family. Whatever you call it, whoever you are, you need one.

—JANE HOWARD,
Families (1978)

Many of us live in highly mobile environments, and moving from place to place takes only minimal thought and preparation. Cars, buses, trains, and planes make travel routine. In our extended families, migration and transition are the norm, and staying connected sometimes takes more energy than we have.

Most Amish women have a very different perspective of family and home. To them stability matters much more than mobility. Why jet to Europe if it means missing the relatives at a reunion? Why move if it fragments families?

Mobility is not something my people need. They long for stable environments and hope to establish roots close to home. Even when they move from one Amish community to another, one of their main priorities is always to protect the integrity of family life, defined not only by the nuclear family but also by the broader network of grandparents, aunts, uncles, and cousins. Letters and frequent visits sustain relationships with those who move away.

Many of us search through long years and many time zones for this kind of steadiness and security. We long for a similar sense of stability. But we look for it in very different ways.

My grandmother lived on the same farm from the day she was born until the day she died. She had very deep roots. I, on the other hand, kept her head spinning as I moved from Pennsylvania to Arkansas to Iowa to Maryland to Florida. She had found her place in the world. I seemed always to be seeking mine.

Modern mobility makes these quests a rite of passage. It is the way we live. A move is an adventure. A better job beckons in a different town or city, and we go. We find a partner in a place far from our family of origin and settle in to make a life. Most of us eventually understand the value and worth of putting down roots, but sometimes it takes many years of searching.

When I came home again in 1987, when I decided to settle among my people in the town where I was born, my life immediately began to change its dimensions. My grandmother was gone, but I know she would have been glad. Glad that all the years of looking for a clan and tribe had brought me back to my home. Glad that I could have a life separate and different from hers, but a life near the places where she lived and nurtured me.

This returning has been a passage I would not have wanted to miss. I reconnected to my parents. I fell in love with my nieces and nephews, a diverse group of young women and men whose lives are a constant source of inspiration and grace. I found links to my extended family of aunts, uncles, and cousins and discovered healing and hope in their stories and voices.

These are the joys of finding a place to call home. Wherever our homes are, may they be places where we feel safe. May the people who live with us surround us with stability, understanding, and unconditional love.

Crime, Punishment, and the Village

The public and the private worlds are inseparably connected. The tyrannies and servilities of the one are the tyrannies and servilities of the other.

—Virginia Woolf,
Three Guineas (1938)

My people suffer. My people come face-to-face with the presence of evil. Perfect communities do not exist, and the Amish subculture is no exception to this rule. It is not free of internal sorrow, wrong, or crime. While an undivided commitment to the way of peace guides most Amish women and men, no depth of commitment isolates them, as it isolates no one, from the darker expressions of human nature.

Growing up, I knew an Amish woman whose chronic problems with shoplifting embarrassed her family and confounded local authorities. Her congregation repeatedly admonished her, begging her to consider the consequences of her actions. She made frequent confessions and worked diligently to overcome the confusion and darkness that drove her behavior.

Amish offenders sometimes perpetrate crimes. Rare accounts of arson, abuse, and even murder plunge my people into deep waves of shock and regret. They accept society's punishments for criminals. They weep. They cry out to God.

"What went wrong?" and "Where did we fail?" are the frequent laments of women and men who feel responsible when an Amish person commits a crime. When touched by these dark impulses of the human spirit, my people respond with disbelief and despair, with pain-filled recognition and introspection.

Perhaps the intensity of the community's reaction helps explain why the Amish produce very few criminals. When I have asked Amish women about criminal activity, their responses have been thoughtful and firm: "We were taught better. We do our best to live with honor and respect and to teach our children the same. Yes, sometimes the young people fall into drinking and even drugs. But to steal from or hurt another person, no. No, that cannot be allowed."

Families, it is believed, bear the primary burden of bringing civilized young people into the community and the world. My people are passionate about the central role of parents. "We can't depend on the church or the school to do our work for us. We are responsible for our children. It's our job to bring them up. To teach them respect for other people and other people's property."

Like many of my people, I have a microcosmic understanding of how to solve the problems of society. No amount of rhetoric changes the world. Hope lies in personal behavior, in the way we treat those close to us. Our children. Our parents. Our friends. Our neighbors. Our families.

In the Amish microcosm, the family stands on the frontier between civilized behavior and crime. I have heard countless Amish women say, "The children need their father, too." Whenever possible both parents, as well as an extended network of grandparents, uncles, and aunts, give the young support. Schools and churches serve as extensions of these homes, the villages so essential to raising children well.

It's a sound system—the Amish way. It produces thousands of healthy, well-adjusted young people. Women and men who begin families of their own and become widely known "as upstanding, honest citizens ready to lend a hand to a neighbor." Who follow in a long tradition of bringing up children "in the fear of God." Who believe their actions make a difference.

We may not always be able to adopt the two-parent, extended family parts of the Amish way, but the system of surrounding ourselves with a community of support is one we might consider. When we're willing to rein in individualism, we can build villages, we can develop communities filled with supportive family members and friends. And in so doing, we influence the world one person, one village, at a time.

Modern Medicine

*T*ime was when medicine could do very little for critically ill or dying patients. Now it can do too much.

—LISA BELKIN,
First, Do No Harm (1993)

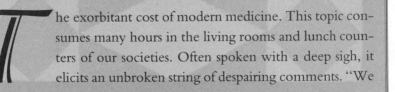

*T*he exorbitant cost of modern medicine. This topic consumes many hours in the living rooms and lunch counters of our societies. Often spoken with a deep sigh, it elicits an unbroken string of despairing comments. "We took Katie in for tests. How can they get away with charging hundreds of dollars for a small procedure?" or "Those pills are two dollars a day, but I can't do without them."

My people also are often exhausted by the excesses of the current medical system. While they ordinarily have no objections to reasonable medical procedures, they are deeply suspicious of costly efforts to extend life.

Amish women disclose highly individual responses to medical intervention. A few suggest sparing no expense in the protection of life. Most draw the line sooner, advocating moderate use of doctors and medical opinions and preferring osteopaths and chiropractors. Others actively avoid doctors, revealing an inclination toward alternative therapies and even a certain vulnerability to quackery. As a group, the Amish church has no rules against modern medicine. Instead, individuals follow their own consciences on this intensely personal issue.

The community does, however, have official positions about insurance and litigation. My people do not permit members to bring lawsuits against medical professionals, no matter how egregious the loss. And they prefer not to carry commercial insurance, relying on each other for help in time of need.

Church leaders advocate with doctors and hospitals for mercy for those encumbered with large bills. They hold public auctions to raise funds. Some communities have even established an internal insurance system called Amish Aid. Without doubt, the Amish attitude about the relative wastefulness of insuring themselves against a *possible* catastrophe has been seriously taxed by the out-of-control costs of modern medicine. Because Amish families and individuals have been bankrupted by medical bills, the community has moderated its position about insurance. Many actively support Amish Aid, and a few have purchased commercial plans.

The story of being bankrupted by medical costs is an all too familiar one. It happens every day to people around us. We live with an extremely inadequate system. We know this, but our hands are tied by those who profit from its craziness.

We might step aside and consider the more simple Amish way. We might begin to support each other in facing the facts of illness, injury, and death. We might refuse expensive procedures that may only prolong life, avoid the temptation to sue for redress—because, in the real world, no amount of money ever relieves our pain—and demand a return to direct, affordable billing practices where we see a doctor and she charges us a reasonable fee for her services.

Yes, many convincing arguments can be made against the relative illogicality of refusing procedures, avoiding lawsuits, and returning to direct billing. But how could the Amish way possibly be less logical than our current system?

Technology and the Amish Community

No one is contented in this world, I believe. There is always something left to desire.
—MARIE CORELLI,
A Romance of Two Worlds (1886)

The twentieth century's advances in technology have, on occasion, invaded the Amish community. Basically a simple folk, content to move slowly and deliberately through the world, many of my people also show a surprising affinity for experimenting with inventions and gadgets. Tractors and cars might be fun. Power lawn mowers certainly take much less energy than push mowers. Personal computers? Wow, what a piece of equipment! These are among the varied responses Amish women and men have to technology.

As enamored by change as many of us, my people also have a healthy mistrust of the supposed magic each new device introduces to the great experiment with modernity. Does the automobile make transportation easier? Did the television revolutionize communication? Does a microwave oven make food comparable to that cooked by wood or gas heat? Will the Internet provide instant access to useful information? Even if the answer to all these questions were yes, Amish women would still ask, "How does that improve your life?"

A valid question, I think, and one worthy of examination. Technology may change our circumstances. It may get us somewhere faster or enable us to have an instantaneous conversation with a person half a world away. But if we expect the quality of our lives to improve because of technology, we will probably be disappointed.

The automobile breaks down, pollutes the environment, and creates traffic jams. The television takes over home life, generating unceasing surveys about the effects of violent programming on kids and teenagers. The microwave beckons us to live on prepackaged foods, costing more money and providing less nutrition. The Internet abounds with information no one needs.

What my people do about technology is ask a simple question: "Will this innovation preserve or threaten our culture?" If it promises to harm the unity or unique qualities of the Amish way, most members willingly live without it. Sometimes, limited use is thought wise. This explains why the Amish hire others to transport them by automobile. Why they use telephones, but relegate them to sheds or barns far from the quiet sanctuary of their homes. Why they accept electric power produced by direct-current 12-volt batteries but reject connections to the 110-volt alternating current of public utility lines.

Amish women know that very few of us would choose to live in a community such as theirs. We love experimenting with the marvelous potential of technology. We would find it hard to wait while the community subjected each invention to a microscopic inspection.

But my people wonder whether our lives might not be less complicated if we at least asked the questions. Will this innovation preserve or threaten the peace and tranquillity of my home? Might I be wiser to adopt some limited form of use? Asking these questions consistently has protected my people and their communities from the many negative aspects of a complete immersion in modernity. If we begin to ask the questions, we may find the answers protecting us and our communities as well.

The Television and Altered Values

We live in an age which must be amused, though genius, feeling, trust, and principle be the sacrifice.
—HANNAH MORE,
"Address to Women of Rank and Fortune" (1799)

Sometimes I watch the morning news shows. If I make it out of bed on time. And if I think I can smile at the sound-bite, perky camaraderie of women and men conversing about the secrets to becoming better, healthier, richer, and, heaven help us, younger.

See this movie. Here's the gorgeous star. Cook this "Oh, that is so delicious!" gourmet dish. (Just once why can't Katie Couric say, "This tastes terrible.") Take these vitamins. Eat carrots. No, don't eat carrots, they're actually bad for you. Do this simple set of exercises every morning. Look, they're so easy, you don't even have to get out of bed.

Don't they know we can tell there's no way the exercise guru keeps herself in perfect shape by kicking her legs up ten times before climbing out of bed? No-o-o. She demonstrates the leg kicks complete with a bed on the set. And the chef bravely cooks shrimp amandine at seven o'clock in the morning. And the doctor makes scary predictions about the dangers of perfectly sane breakfast foods like milk and eggs.

Why do they do it? Because we lap it up. We tune in and stay tuned. We go out and see the movies. We buy the exercise videos and the shrimp, garlic, and vermouth. We make ambitious resolutions to eat more healthfully and stay younger. That is, until the next morning or evening when real life sets in. We're too tired to kick up our legs and too weary to dash off gourmet shrimp dinners. We settle for soup, cellulite, and the companionship of a husband, pet, or good friend. All of which we and the morning shows might want to spend more time celebrating.

Amish women don't have televisions. They don't watch these shows. Nor do they understand the vernacular. Women such as my mother are convinced they would jeopardize their value systems if they allowed TVs in their homes. Whenever I comment about the absurdity of something I've seen, my mother is more than likely to say, "Well, now see, that's just exactly why we don't have one of those things. I think you'd be better off without it, too."

Staying forever healthy, rich, and young holds no charm in Amish society, where older people are treasured and revered for their wisdom and generosity. Where entertainment revolves around the simplest joys of life—visiting with friends, reading books, playing ball, singing hymns, or taking long walks in the woods. And where values are not determined or altered by the snazziest lifestyle, the latest predictions, or the newest trends.

Few of us will follow my mother's advice and get rid of our TVs. But we might be wise to remind ourselves that television is a two-dimensional source of information. It can never compete with real life, where every situation has many dimensions. Where it is often healthier to eat lots of eggs and carrots. Where it is sometimes safer and even sexier to be a few pounds overweight. Where it is more fun to stay home than to go to the movies.

LOUISE STOLTZFUS

❧ ❧

Giving In to Contentment

*T*wo people cannot see things from the same point of view, and the slightest difference in angle changes the thing seen.

—MILDRED ALDRICH,
A Hilltop on the Marne (1915)

life of yieldedness. This is what many women among my people strive for. Instead of quarreling with God, they give in. Instead of indulging themselves, they surrender their desires to the good of the community. Instead of biting back, they turn the other cheek to those who hurt them. Instead of wanting more, they seek to be content with what they have.

Why quarrel with God? As women of the world, we have many different philosophies about the nature of God. The principles we learn in childhood may not sustain our adult experiences. We are left with a stream of questions that have no simple answers.

My people view God through the lens of their community. God's requests are made clear to them by a reading of the Holy Bible and by the wisdom of those called to preach the gospel. When the two agree, that is, when the words of the preacher agree with the words of the Bible, women among my people feel little need to quarrel with God. They quietly give in and devote themselves to lives of faithfulness.

While our people groups and religious understandings may be different, many of us also find God in community. In such cooperative revelations of God, we find the comfort and mercy that frees us from quarreling with God.

Why indulge ourselves? The self-gratification of individual satisfaction grips many of us in a succession of questionable behaviors and choices. We drink too much. We eat too much. We forget about others in the exploration of personal accomplishment. My people view self-indulgence as harmful to their gathered life. Often after long debate and careful consideration, they let go of their desire for things like electric lights or personal recognition to keep the peace, as they say, among the people.

They are certain: There is a direct link between self-indulgence and hostility. To insist on having one's own way hinders the happiness and disturbs the peace of the community. If others have listened to your reasons and heard your stories, it is often wiser to give in. Not without debate. But always to preserve the tranquillity of a home, friendship, or neighborhood.

Why turn the other cheek? This hard teaching of Jesus and its distinct image of not fighting back has raised questions throughout the ages. My people do not interpret it literally. To stand before a person who is actually beating you and turn the other cheek is seen by all reasonable Amish women and men as an inaccurate way of understanding Jesus. What this means to women among my people is more accurately depicted in the advice of my grandmother: "When someone picks a fight with you, walk away. Do not fight back."

An overwhelmingly difficult choice in a world torn by conflict and strife, walking away takes courage and discipline. But, without doubt, my grandmother had an insight worth remembering—one way to disengage a bully is to leave the scene of the fight.

How do we seek contentment? Many of us struggle with great windstorms of personal desire that toss us from fencerow to tree, from earth to sky and back again. My people suggest rushing for basements or closets when the storms of want threaten to undo the gentle breezes of being good to ourselves. In those shelters, let us give in to contentment; let us relax and let the wind blow around us.

Friendship for the Ages

Whither thou goest, I will go;
And where thou lodgest, I will lodge;
Thy people shall be my people.
And thy God my God.

—*Book of Ruth*

*I*t is often friendship that holds the world together. The ageless Old Testament account of Ruth's friendship with her mother-in-law, Naomi, inspires each new generation of readers. It is the story of two women, bonded by the death of Ruth's husband (Naomi's son), and their journey through a lifelong friendship. A friendship that overcame the odds of age, culture, and distance. A friendship that nurtured both women through the shadows of suffering and the full flowering of happiness. A friendship for the ages.

My people know this story, and they plant, tend, and water the same gardens of companionship among themselves. Most Amish women consider one other woman a best friend and have a wider circle of peers often identified as "my group of friends." They meet regularly, sometimes spontaneously, although seldom without giving notice.

"When we get together, we sit around and visit. We drink coffee and eat. Maybe something has happened to someone, and we all give her a chance to talk. Sometimes you just need to talk." That is how Lydia describes a gathering of friends at her house. "I also have a very close friend. We used to get together once a month, but she married and moved farther away. Now she drops a postcard every once in a while to tell me she's coming for a visit. She likes when I pamper her for a day because she has lots of children and grandchildren now, and she just needs someone to do for her sometimes, too."

We, the women of the world, face many barriers to the warmth and richness of friendship. We are too busy. It takes work to get together. We just don't have time. We need to be more present for our husbands, partners, or families.

How is it, I sometimes ask myself, that I have managed to turn this essential exercise of human kindness into work? How is it, we may all want to ask, that we have time and money to visit and pay therapists when a regularly maintained friendship might offer the same support and much greater reward? How is that we have permitted telephone or "chat room" online communication to replace the near eyes of a loved one, the comfort of touch, and the treasure of a great friendship?

My people are sure that movies and restaurants are not essential to the activity of friendship. They take walks. Stitch quilts. Bake bread. Meet in each other's homes for coffee and conversation.

It is, after all, togetherness, not entertainment, that is so often lost in the bustle of our busy days. We may need no more than the gentle stroke of another woman's voice and hands to reduce the stress in our lives and to remind us that nothing, not even a wonderful man, is worth the squandering of a great friendship.

Boaz, the charming landowner to whom Ruth gave herself, came to love Naomi as much as Ruth. Ruth and Boaz's marriage produced children, cherished by two women whose story of friendship has brought blessing and hope to many future generations.

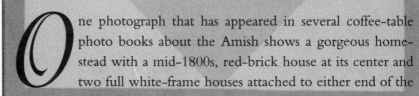

Architectural Gems and Old Age

Ripe old age, cheerful, useful, and understanding, is one of the finest influences in the world.
—IDA TARBELL,
The Business of Being a Woman (1912)

One photograph that has appeared in several coffee-table photo books about the Amish shows a gorgeous homestead with a mid-1800s, red-brick house at its center and two full white-frame houses attached to either end of the original structure. The roof lines, window arrangements, and dimensions of the frame additions accent the old house and create a pleasing architectural whole. I have seen this house many times, and it is a gem.

It is also a home with a story. A story about reverence for senior citizens and the wisdom that comes with old age. A story about my people and their way with those who are growing old. There are many, many homes like this in Amish country. Lovely and palatial in presentation, they are both symbolic and real. Real because they provide great-grandparents, grandparents, and, on occasion, single aunts and uncles a place to live out their days. Symbolic because they support a belief system that cares for its own.

Among my people, retirement, or slowing down, as the Amish prefer to call this transition, begins early. Parents as young as the late forties or early fifties often turn over day-to-day farm or small business operations to a married son or daughter. These vibrant, fifty-something, middle-aged women and men want the younger generation to have a chance at making their own way in the world. They step aside. But they do not fade away.

"We slow down to enjoy life, but we don't retire." Few ever retire. They lead productive lives until the end, often still planting fields, carpentering, cooking, or quilting into their eighties and nineties. Old age is not a burden. Nor is it something my people seek to deny or to avoid. Gray hair, lines across the forehead, and stooped shoulders are distinguishing marks of knowledge and wisdom. Few consider moving to a milder climate. Grandparents stay close because "the young people need us." Many go no further than "the other end of the house," as the classic additions to their homes are often called.

In the summer of 1886, my father's mother was born in a bedroom of one such American manor house on her father's family farm. When she married in 1911, this slight, strong woman inherited the farm and raised her children in its spacious environs. She lived well—gardening, sewing, canning, and moving about the farm. At age ninety-nine, she died peacefully during an Amish church service in the house where she was born. We all say she could not have lived a better life.

For Amish women such as my grandmother, growing old often enhances and enlarges life experience. The hard work of raising a family and making a living mellows as these women settle in to enjoy the "fruits of their labor." They read. Sometimes, they travel. They cherish their grandchildren. They help their neighbors and friends.

Children and young people are taught that the older ones have life learnings and wisdom that they need to seek out, to hear, and to heed. And busy young fathers and mothers turn to their wiser parents for advice and support during the sometimes troubling years of providing for a family.

The lonely, institutional corridors of retirement communities and nursing homes do not exist in the Amish experience. Although this sometimes adds a temporary burden when an older family member becomes ill, the blessings far outweigh the struggles.

Our American society, with its isolated, single-family, suburban homes, has moved a long way from this model of care for the aging members of our families. An emphasis on individual nuclear families prevents most of us from considering the Amish way. But there are some among us who have taken up the challenge of urging our parents to stay close to us.

I live in an inner-city urban community. Several years ago, my friends Michael and Alonna helped his parents find a home on our block. The shared baby-sitting, snow shoveling, and gardening benefits three generations and provides a more secure foundation for the three young children of this family. Wherever we may live and whatever the limitations of our own arrangements, we can learn from the Amish way, from its reverence for those who have grown old.

LOUISE STOLTZFUS

❧ ❧

The Grandmother's Place

*T*hy children like the olive branches:
round about thy table.
—*Book of Psalms*

any Amish women really enjoy being grandmothers. The sometimes uneven rhythms of raising children slowly yield to the more even rhythms of nurturing grandchildren. The worries are fewer. The joys are more. That is what Malinda thinks. She has nine children and forty-seven grandchildren.

When I ask her to describe a typical day, she says, "Well, my days just aren't so typical, since I have grandchildren. Sometimes I think I'll start spring housecleaning or maybe do some quilting, but then one of the girls drops in with the babies."

Malinda, who is sixty-seven, and her sixty-eight-year-old husband devote countless hours to the care and nurture of their grandchildren. About ten years ago, they retired from the family farm, built an addition to the farmhouse, and turned the sixty acres of land over to their youngest son. He moved with his new wife into the original house.

These days the homestead gleams, alive with gorgeous flowers and bouncing grandchildren. Their son grows potted wholesale flowers in his fields. And his children love nothing more than slipping over to see *Mummy* and *Dawdy*. "All our children like to come home. And we like it when they come."

As I hear Malinda's gentle descriptions of life among her grand-children, I remember how much I used to love being near my Amish grandparents. How much I longed to visit them. How much I still long for them. I think people like Malinda and my grandparents, with their high regard for children and childhood, challenge us with their shining testimonials of dedicating themselves to the care and keeping of the next generation.

These are people who pay little attention to money or success. They advise each other to make do with what they have and to cut corners and save wherever they can. To these women and men, the height of fulfillment is watching their children and grandchildren lead happy, well-adjusted lives. When the adjustments lose their alignment, as they sometimes do, they stand and stay nearby, willing to give whatever advice the child or grandchild needs to restore wellness.

Many a young Amish mother has been immeasurably revived by a long conversation with her mother or mother-in-law over a cup of tea or coffee. "I think that's part of the grandmother's job,"

Malinda tells me, "to listen to them." I think she is so wise and so right.

It is something most of us can do. We may not have nine and forty-seven, but the children and grandchildren we do have still need our care and keeping. Our unconditional love. Not our condemnation. Just our love.

What I Learned from My Grandmother about Love

The memories of long love
gather like drifting snow.
—LADY MURASAKI,
The Tale of Genji (c. 1008)

We could not have been more than maybe three, four, and five—my brothers and I. On that warm and distant summer evening as we jumped and skipped on the spacious front lawn of my grandparents' home. Suddenly, there they were. A glorious array of glittering fireflies buzzing a few feet above the freshly mown grass. We grabbed them with glee and came running, fists tightly closed and faces eager to display our treasures.

As always, she had an idea. The tender woman we called *Mummy*. *"Oh die kleine, kummet doh rivvah. Ich mach euch eppes fah sie ketcha"* (Oh my dear ones, come over here. I'll fix you something to catch them). And away she went to punch holes in the lid of an empty canning jar, bringing it back and laughing through the twilight with my parents and grandfather as we raced back and forth between them, the canning jar, and the firefly-lighted grounds.

Often since, on summer evenings, I have remembered as I've watched my mother do the same for her grandchildren. It's such a classic grandmother thing to do. And one of the finest and fullest memories I have of a woman whose life was devoted to her children and grandchildren.

LOUISE STOLTZFUS

❀ ❀

Devoted to surrounding us with acceptance and love. When she died, I was thirty-four years old with a budding career vastly different from anything she could ever have imagined for me. But in her heart, I was still the little girl she had called to her side and helped to catch fireflies. The little girl, the young woman, she loved.

She asked me hard questions in the last years, listening carefully to my answers, welcoming my perspective, and sometimes smiling briefly at my passion and purpose. Eventually, she could no longer talk. Then she would raise her eyebrows ever so slightly at the distant woman I had become. They dropped quickly whenever I laughed and admitted how strange the path I had taken must seem to her.

I could never say she approved of my life's choices. I can only say she loved me. I can only say she extended an unconditional faith across the divide. Across the differences we felt because she had given a rich and full life to being Amish, and I was not following in her footsteps.

Ours is a story repeated among women everywhere. Whether we are homemakers whose daughters wish to be poets and writers and singers. Whether we are artists whose daughters wish to be wives and mothers. Whether we are women whose daughters wish to be our mirror images. No matter where they go or what they do, we have an eternal obligation to their souls. To love them forever.

As we come to these crossroads with our daughters and grand-daughters, as we watch them reaching for lifeways we cannot comprehend, may we be as wise as my grandmother. May we ask them questions. May we listen to their answers and stories. May we extend them comfort and love. May we in all things be faithful, to ourselves and to each other.

LOUISE STOLTZFUS

🌺 🌺

Epilogue

At the core of every soul, in the essence of every people, lies a deep well of truth that informs everything we learn and believe about ourselves, our people, and the world around us. It is the source of integrity, the genesis of courage, the essential reason that guides a faithful life. This is what I learned from my people—the Amish women whose nature and nourishing permeated my personal narrative.

My story is not original. It is repeated over and over again as we, the women of the world, reconnect to the people, places, and things that illuminate our lives. For it is in the folkways and family legends that guide and inspire our individual dreams and hopes that we are most likely to find the truth that will keep us on paths of faithfulness.

That is where this road back to my people has taken me—to the simple ways of the women who raised me. In their quiet reverence for the eternal qualities of life and their sincere celebration of the everyday, my people have taught me to treasure the limitless power of God, to cherish the natural order of the world, and to live well with both of these truths. They have reminded me to believe in myself, to demonstrate confidence and trust in the great mysteries of life.

I have not always succeeded. I will not always succeed. But I will always know it has been the same for them. Though they, too, have failed from time to time, they have returned again and again to the well of their truth. So can I.

In listening to their intricate and many-layered stories, I have remembered the wisdom of being separate from the whims and wishes of the world. The fast and furious pace of modernity has sometimes taken me far from my home. But this returning has renewed my spirit and my faith.

For simple pleasure cannot be isolated from faithfulness. Whether it is momentary or infinite, the experience of pleasure expects and requires of each of us a certain expression of faith. A certain regard for those with whom we participate in the adventurous and daring explorations of contentment, fulfillment, and satisfaction.

Most of us eventually realize that we will never change the world.

LOUISE STOLTZFUS

❀ ❀

What we must quickly go on to learn, if we wish to be solid and sound, may well be the essential truth that most affects who we are and how we will be remembered—the way we live may not change the world, but it absolutely does make a difference for those whose lives we touch. Because of this truth, we must determine to be faithful to ourselves and to each other. Whether we choose to be selfish or selfless, detached or present, thoughtful or thoughtless, our conduct will affect and ultimately change the way those close to us experience the world. From my people, I have learned that returning to the heart of one's personal narrative helps assure that those changes will be healing and regenerative.

This journey to the center of our own stories is never easy. It asks of each of us a lifetime of patience and practice. It is filled with moments of failure, but also with years of success. Whatever failure or success arises in the course of the journey, we cannot abandon our own well of truth—a well that offers not only the source of self-awareness, but also the source of simplicity and easy living.

Everything I hold dear about my people is linked to the serene and simple pleasures of faithfulness in family and home, in business and community. Living without these pleasures is like the lingering sadness of a last kiss, like being let go too soon, like losing a friend. Living with these pleasures is like the exquisite memory of a first kiss, like being held long and well, like being forever with an old companion.

In the frenzied and fragmented environment that defines so much of the world today, many of us yearn for this kind of simplicity. I have found it in the homespun philosophies, in the faithful renderings, of my people. I have found it in their words of kindness and mercy. I have found it in their gifts of compassion and love, freely given and freely received.

I believe that each of us may find equal measures of peace and understanding, of mystery and wisdom, as we return to and draw from the wells that supply life-affirming and life-giving sustenance to our people, to our homes, to our many and varied personal narratives.

LOUISE STOLTZFUS

❦ ❦

Translation of *"O Gott Vater,"* page 145:

> Our Father God, thy name we praise
> To thee our hymns addressing,
> And joyfully our voices raise
> Thy faithfulness confessing;
> Assembled by thy grace, O Lord,
> We seek fresh guidance from thy word.
> Now grant anew thy blessing!

About the Author

Louise Stoltzfus lives in Lancaster, Pennsylvania, ten miles from her ancestral home. She is the author of *Amish Women: Lives and Stories* (1994) and *Two Amish Folk Artists: The Story of Henry Lapp and Barbara Ebersol* (1995). She has also written or co-written six recipe collections, including *Favorite Recipes from Quilters* and *The Central Market Cookbook*.